D1557569

Introduction to Chinese History

Introduction to Chinese History

From Ancient Times to 1912

BODO WIETHOFF

WESTVIEW PRESS · BOULDER, COLORADO

Translated from the German
Grundzüge der älteren chinesischen Geschichte
by Mary Whittall

Published in 1975 in the United States of America
by Westview Press, Inc.
  1898 Flatiron Court
  Boulder, Colorado 80301
  Frederick A. Praeger, Publisher and Editorial Director

Library of Congress Cataloging in Publication Data
Wiethoff, Bodo.
  Introduction to Chinese history.

  Translation of Grundzüge der älteren
chinesischen Geschichte.
  Bibliography: p.
  Includes index.
  1. China—History. I Title.
DS736.W4713 951   75–25694
ISBN 0-89158-516-8

Printed in Great Britain

CONTENTS

Preface

Confining itself to the ancient and traditional state which ended constitutionally in 1912, this book aims to provide an introduction to the history of China. In dealing with Chinese history since the abdication in that year of the last Ch'ing emperor, a completely separate approach seems necessary, in view of that history's complexity, terms of reference, and what is perhaps a quite different structure – though admittedly the origins of the modern state may be sought in the traditional era and past traditions can be regarded as surviving for a time.

Chronological listing of events plays a relatively small part in the presentation of the subject. The history of ancient and traditional China stretches over approximately three thousand years and comprises an almost unsurpassable amount of detailed information. Anything like a thorough presentation of that immense continuum would be quite beyond the scope of this book. Above all, it devotes less attention to individual acts and events than to typical structures. The separate chapters are concerned with structures and tendencies typical of Chinese history, and it is socio-political aspects, the evolution of the social forms of China, that will chiefly engage our attention. Literary and artistic developments, as well as most other forms of expression regarded as integral components of Chinese life, will hardly be mentioned.

The absence of footnotes and a list of sources is due to lack of space. The bibliography consists of a selection of the most essential and accessible works, arranged according to chapter divisions, but including only those in European languages.

1 Historiography

History is, in the broadest sense, change in time; history is also the depiction of this change. History as the empirical essence of things and history as reflection form a dialectical unit, formulated in words. History is events, too, but these cannot be objectified in the same way; history 'does not make a gift of itself' (Heuss). In other words, history consciously recognized as such has already undergone a transformation, according to what could be called the first principle of historical alienation. This is characteristic of historical reflection within a given unit, whether national or universal. Certainly it applies to Chinese history, discoverable as it is behind very nearly all the earlier sources. But everything on these pages was written by a European, not a Chinese, and therefore emanates from a different historical viewpoint and a different historical background. Before approaching the subject directly, therefore, it is necessary to outline the way in which Chinese history has been received and reflected in Europe in the past. The different effects of motivation and intention on historical reflection could be called the second principle of historical alienation. This twofold alienation cannot be overlooked in writing about Chinese history: it is an integral part of it.

CHINA'S HISTORY THROUGH EUROPEAN EYES

The earliest European accounts of China were not historical, but tales of travellers like the Italian Franciscan Giovanni de Piano Carpini, who was at the court of the Mongol khan in 1246, the Flemish Franciscan William of Rubruk, who visited the Mongol capital of Karakorum in 1254, and the Venetian Marco Polo, who was in Mongolia and China from 1275 to 1292. Neither of the two friars actually got to China itself, and so their rather brief remarks about that distant land include some fantastic material that was presumably common currency in central Asia at that date. William of Rubruk says at one point, for instance, that he has it on good authority that one city in China actually has walls of silver and gold. But Marco Polo, too, who lived in China itself for many years and went on several long journeys through the country, described the empire as flourishing, a merchant's paradise with widespread prosperity. In so far as his accounts were not decried as fanciful boasting, they left the West with the impression that China was the richest and most prosperous land in the world.

Such was also the general tenor of the reports of the second wave of European travellers, who reached China in the sixteenth century, such as the Portuguese Galeote Pereira, who was a prisoner in China from 1549 to 1552, Gaspar da Cruz, another Portuguese who visited China in 1556, and the Spanish Augustinian friar Martin de Rada, who visited the province of Fukien in 1575. But their journeys were motivated by different considerations. The thirteenth-century friars, and the Polos too, on their second journey, had been commissioned by the Curia to negotiate a military alliance with the Mongols against Islam. The sixteenth-century travellers were sent by the mercantile nations that had risen to power in Europe in the meantime, as official ambassadors and trade delegates. One of their aims was the Christian mission, the others were trade and picking up useful information. De Rada was instructed, among other things, to find out as much as possible about the country and its people, both what was freely available and what was kept secret, but above all to learn about their trade, whether they were reliable partners and what goods were available for exchange.

De Rada's highly informative report was the first to include a short historical survey. Together with accounts from the many other European travellers of the sixteenth century, it provided the basis of the first major European book about China, the *Historia de las cosas mas notables, ritos y costumbres, del gran reyno de China*, by a Spanish Augustinian, Juan Gonzáles de Mendoza. This was translated into almost every European language and determined the European view of China for a long time to come. An English version was published in London in 1588 (*The Historie of the great and mightie kingdome of China, and the situation thereof: togither with the great riches, huge citties, politike gouernment, and rare inuentions in the same.* Translated out of the Spanish by R. Parke) and a German edition in 1589.

10

The Jesuit missionaries of the seventeenth century added a new dimension to European knowledge of China. History and religious matters had previously been treated cursorily, but the learned fathers of the Society of Jesus devoted their full attention to them. They sought the causes for the unique public order and prosperity of China, and they also wanted to establish correct intellectual premises for their mission, aimed at the educated stratum of Chinese society. Somewhat later, too, came the need to justify their own missionary concept by historical argument. The Jesuit mission was pioneered in China by Matteo Ricci, from 1583 to 1610. From the first his principal goal, and that of the tradition he founded, was the conversion of the emperor, in the sure hope that the rest of the country would follow. Ricci very soon realized that belittling the nature of Chinese religious beliefs, an apparent prerequisite, would be problematical in itself. But his investigations convinced him that their rites were basically no more than expressions of reverence and respect and that they therefore did not come into conflict with Christian ideas. The Jesuits were so successful in China that they soon had almost a monopoly of missionary activity in the empire. This was a privilege which, allied with their tolerance of Chinese rituals, earned them violent criticism on the part of their clerical and secular enemies. One of their defences was the historical argument: not so much political history, to begin with, as the traditional Chinese ideas about God, morals and belief. In 1687 a group of Jesuits published Confucian texts for the first time in the West, under the title *Confucius Sinarum Philosophus*, and in 1696 Father Louis Le Comte, in his *Nouveaux Mémoires sur la Chine*, went so far as to assert that the Chinese had known and worshipped the True God for more than two thousand years, providing an example that could well be followed by Christendom. Not surprisingly this claim aroused a storm in Europe.

The publications of members of other orders did nothing to create a clearer or more acceptable picture of China, past or present. Martin Martini's *Sinicae Historicae Decas Prima* of 1658, for instance, revealed that the official Chinese chronology began a good six hundred years earlier than the date of Noah's Flood, reckoned according to the Vulgate, the only version of the Bible then acknowledged in Catholic Europe, and that it therefore appeared to bear out the older Septuagint. *Tratados historicos, politicos, ethicos y religiosos de la Monarchia de China*, published in 1676 by the Spanish Dominican Domingo Fernandez Navarrete, gave rise to similar

11

confusion over fundamental questions. Navarrete was already exploring historical sources, whose authenticity has only been recognized again recently. As far as is known he was the first European to draw attention to the wealth of historical information in the *Local Gazetteers* (*fang-chih*). The Jesuit Antoine Gaubil (1689–1759) also made a study of informative, reliable primary sources, notably the *Veritable Records* (*shih-lu*), a category of source material that is closer to historical events than the official histories. Gaubil wanted to present Chinese history and the writing of ancient and modern Chinese historians in an accurate and critical light, but his work, too, was coloured by ideological controversies in Europe. Russia also saw the publication of books about China from the seventeenth century onwards, but once again contemporary preoccupations filled the foreground, for instance in the *Description of the first part of the Universe, called Asia, which includes the State of China . . .* by Nikolay Milesku Spafary (1636–1708), and the study of the Manchurian Banner detachments by Ilarion Kalinovich Rossokhin (1717–61).

Two works in particular fixed European conceptions of Chinese history for decades to come: Jean Baptiste du Halde's *Description géographique, historique, chronologique, politique et physique de l'empire de la Chine et de la Tartarie chinoise*, published in 1735, and Joseph François Marianne de Moyriac de Mailla's *Histoire général de la Chine, ou Annales de cet Empire*, published between 1777 and 1783. Du Halde was the editor of *Lettres édifiantes et curieuses écrites des missions étrangères par quelques missionaires de la compagnie de Jésus*, published from 1702 onwards; his book was essentially assembled from the excellent descriptions of China given in these letters, typical of the high standards of Jesuit reporting. De Mailla's text, on the other hand, paraphrased one of the most influential Chinese works of historical literature, the twelfth-century *Outlines and Details* based on the *Comprehensive Mirror* by Chu Hsi. This was less a descriptive work of history than a textbook of political morals along Neo-Confucian lines. De Mailla's *Histoire générale* was not published until thirty years after completion. Its publication, like that of the *Mémoires concernant l'histoire, les sciences, les arts, les moeurs et les usages des Chinois par les Missionaires de Pékin* between 1776 and 1814, represented the Jesuits' last great effort to salvage their own credibility and – ostensibly their primary concern, but in fact incidentally – the picture of China as an ideal society. They achieved exactly the opposite and provided the soil in which there grew up a historiographical tradition banishing China, apparently at her own wish, from world history.

The European estimation of China changed when progress became the paramount criterion of human history. To begin with, this concept was given no historical foundation, but 'revolutionary intellectuals' saw it as a polemical rebuttal of the absolutism dominating European thought in the eighteenth century; with the passage of time the ensuing industrial, scientific and political revolution appeared to justify it. Against this background, Chinese history was judged by criteria taken not from that history, but from the concept that contemporary Europe had of itself. Progressive thinkers of the eighteenth and nineteenth centuries accepted the image of China propagated so enthusiastically by the Jesuits – the myth of the homogeneous Confucian state, the timeless perpetuation of the great ideals apparently realized in Chinese society – and interpreted it in a different light. What the Jesuits regarded as evidence of a successfully organized society was to the progressives proof of the inferiority of that society and the superiority of their own.

This change in European attitudes took place at the turn of the eighteenth century, and was influenced above all by German philosophers. Johann Gottfried Herder, who divided the world into 'schön gebildete' and 'nicht schön gebildete' (cultivated and uncultivated) races, accepted as proven the long-standing existence of all the institutions and characteristics of China and the Chinese people, and attributed it to their 'Mongolian origins'.

> The empire is an embalmed mummy, painted with hieroglyphs and swaddled in silk; its circulation has the sluggish vitality of animals in hibernation. ... Fate has placed the people of China in a corner of the earth, remote from the stimulating contacts between other nations, shutting them away behind mountains, deserts and an almost impenetrable coastline.

These two features, lack of development and remoteness, governed European opinions of China and its history in the nineteenth century. Hegel spoke of the Chinese as a race which had 'really no history'. China, for him, was the exception to his theory of evolution that proved the rule. Let it be said that Hegel formed his opinion in good faith. Referring to the 'very learned men who studied China in the eighteenth century' and the 'isolated' Chinese who had come to Europe, he believed that he could truly claim 'that we now know all there is to be known about China and that we are now as well informed about her literature and her life as about her history'. Ranke numbered the Chinese among the 'races of eternal stasis'. In his view only those nations which had evolved a 'unique, unified cultural world' out of the separate currents of their own historical development, qualified as the subjects of a 'world history'. The young Marx, too, regarded China as a 'carefully preserved mummy in a hermetically sealed coffin', while Friedrich Engels apostrophized it as a 'decaying semi-culture at the end of the earth', with hardly a claim to any historical interest. In the opinion of most of the European historical philosophers of the nineteenth century it was only in Europe that history took the form of purposeful evolution. Evolution was linear, irreversible and not liable to repetition. Where there was repetition, as was obviously the case in China, there could be no history. This conviction was a correlative of European imperial ambitions, and appeared confirmed by the successes of imperialism. With this premiss, Hegel could argue with impeccable logic that Asia did not begin to take part in history until the moment when it was first visited and explored. The Englishman Edward H. Parker expressed this view more bluntly in 1901: 'The human interest in Chinese history begins with their foreign relations'; in other words, in the nineteenth century. Chinese history before then he dismissed as 'wearisome', 'insipid' and 'downright stupid'. Again, writing in the *North China Herald* in 1908, another Englishman, Arthur H. Smith, declared that there was every reason why the world in general should concern itself as little with Chinese history as it did: 'Chinese history is remote, monotonous, obscure and, worst of all, there is too much of it.'

In spite of general opinion, some nineteenth-century European scholars did go on with research into Chinese history. Much of their work was speculative, such as that of Terrien de Lacouperie (1845–94), who interpreted Chinese culture as a variant of Near Eastern civilization, and the Chinese people as related to the peoples of Mesopotamia. Other publications, such as those of the American Orientalists, were inspired by missionary zeal and an eagerness to justify the writers' own self-satisfaction. Yet others were painstaking in their philology, but anecdotal and fragmentary in their content, such as those by Johann Heinrich Platz (1802–74) and August Pfizmaier (1808–87). The study of Chinese history according to the precepts of European scholarship increased rather than lessened towards the end of the nineteenth century. The first journal of sinology, *T'oung Pao*, founded in 1890, acted as a clearing house. But with it there also began the tradition that still dominated sinology, once nicknamed 'micro-sinology' by the American historian J. K. Fairbank, of 'establishing textual facts for facts' sake'. Chinese history, however, largely continued to be ignored by other historians, so that as late as 1919 it was still possible for the classical historian Eduard Schwartz to write: 'What is known as Chinese historiography is just Chinese to me, incomprehensible in other words. But why should Europeans know anything about Chinese history, when even the Sinologists have dismissed it as uninteresting?'

But the typically Eurocentric view of history may not have been the only reason for the dismissal of Chinese history. In China, unlike Africa, America and Australia, European expansionism, which was always intellectual expansionism as well, came up against a pre-existing historical consciousness that was not easily dispelled. China was not to be incorporated in the historical process in the same way as other objects of European imperialism. Only two reactions were possible towards China and Chinese history: total rejection or, as in the past, acceptance as valuable exemplars. The choice made did not depend on China and her history, however, but on the current state of the European consciousness.

The first decades of the twentieth century witnessed a change in that consciousness. Europe was suddenly made aware of China again as a historical reality and potentiality, precisely when European world dominance began to wane. New combinations of circumstances arose in Asia, as Japan grew in strength and China itself embarked on the process of radical reshaping, which compelled a closer look at their origins. The philosophical advance into the truly universal dimension of history had a retroflective effect, lending a new sense of immediacy and relevance to the remote and uninteresting pasts of the countries in question. As Karl Jaspers said later, it was no longer possible to dismiss the great nations of Asia as peoples without history, eternally static. Oswald Spengler was one of the earliest to share the new interest in China, but he formed no new image of it. For Spengler, China was still a petrified relic, the model of a post-historic society. Similarly Arnold Toynbee: his *Study of History* includes a detailed consideration of China, and numerous individual developments in Chinese history confirm his thesis of the universal dialectic of challenge and response as the motive force of history. But in the end he too interprets the inertia of traditional China as petrifaction, the end of a road. Historical sociologists also found China a useful point of reference at this period, especially Max Weber. He aimed to pinpoint identifying characteristics of European structures, which he assumed to be universally significant, but this seemed possible only via analysis of other cultural systems. Weber believed that comparison offered the only means of 'forming a more clearly focused view of the genesis of the unique historical nature of European cultural development'. In his later works Weber was concerned exclusively with the special position of modern European capitalism and the related unique rationality of European technology, intellectual disciplines, society and political institutions. Studies such as these of Weber and Toynbee played a part in drawing Chinese history to the attention of the non-sinologists again; but forced it into new schemata likewise originating in specific European standpoints. The act of including China in historical comparisons and citing it as proof of this or that historical case, demonstrates that the cognition of data from a history not one's own, like the recollection of one's own tradition in a period pre-dating the academic study of history, will always go to confirm one's pre-conceptions.

On the one hand, therefore, China provided a convenient object of comparison for theories of universal history and sociological structuring. On the other, its history was starting to be uncovered piecemeal in isolated researches. It was against this background that Otto Franke undertook the first comprehensive history of China based on Chinese sources. It was the first time, too, that a European historian took as his guiding theme a principle implicit in Chinese historical tradition.

> Among no other race in the world are the social order, the customary and moral relationships between individuals, the total outlook on life itself, more unanimously and incontrovertibly rooted in the one concept that already contains all these in itself in embryo, that is in the concept of family and state.

Franke was influenced by a preference for the officially sanctioned Chinese histories, in which the Confucian view of family and state occupied a position of central importance. He was also probably affected by the nineteenth-century conviction that the state was the central subject of history. Franke sought to make more widely known the immense store of human experience contained in Chinese history; but he also wanted to see China take her place among the 'world nations', as defined by Ranke. In spite of recent changes, he also believed it possible to take the 'uniformity of the historical and cultural development of China' as a starting point, and to use the

16

'present to illuminate the past' in order to reveal the 'true inter-relationships of the facts'. This basis simply will not serve today for a history of China. Another of Franke's premisses, that human beings all over the world are moved by essentially the same forces, passions and urges, is debatable. We may accept that man as a physical genus is everywhere the same, but the identity may not include his historical or social being. Not a great deal is known of the historical psychology of the Chinese, for instance. Research has barely started into the rudimentary conceptions and categorizations, the priorities of everyday life, the sense of space and time, the attitudes to work, leisure and play. Yet factors like these, which are formed by history, are at least as relevant historically as general human attributes.

But if Otto Franke was still guided essentially by the image of Chinese history presented in traditional sources, his successors, and indeed some of his contemporaries, increasingly turned their backs on it. New guiding principles and categorization systems, based as before, however, on European preconceptions and academic tenets, were brought to bear on the Chinese sources; they were scrutinized for what they could offer of interest to ethnology, technology, economic history, political science and sociology. This phase of sinology had already started before the Second World War; but the post-war changes in world politics greatly increased general interest in Chinese history. 'China's entry into the ranks of the great powers and the victory of Communism are not the kind of events to be shrugged off as taking place at the end of the world' (Herbert Franke). The origins of the new China, and the clues their discovery may give to the nation's future course, have become a more urgent field of research than in the early years of the century. Whether the study of Chinese history will be able to provide a satisfactory account of those origins is uncertain, but it is a task that it cannot evade. The study of history cannot concern itself with antiquarianism alone but must always offer guidelines for the future as well. Naturally the task is regarded as most urgent in countries whose confrontation with China is most direct: the United States and the Soviet Union. In his recent programmatic 'Tasks for the Seventies', J. K. Fairbank underlined the need for a comprehensive study of Chinese history with a view to a completely new orientation of the American relationship with the Far East. Current preoccupations, political as well as ideological, always governed the Soviet view of China in the past and, just as in western Europe, Chinese history was interpreted according to the ruling

17

conceptions of international and internal affairs. Discussion in the 1930s was dominated by ideologically important questions such as the nature of the 'Asiatic mode of production'. After the war, when many Asian states had gained independence, or, like China, had embarked on a new course, interest grew and became more specialized. Regional studies were promoted and extended, with particular attention being paid to the ideologically and politically important fields of social and economic history, revolutionary history and the history of the Asian minority races and the inhabitants of border areas between larger neighbours. Recently Soviet sinologists have extended their interest yet further, to embrace the state and laws, philosophy and culture, on the grounds that a purely economic viewpoint does not define the circumstances adequately.

The intensity and quality of Western interest in China have always been functions of Europe's image of itself. Sino-history and sinology as a whole seem always to have flourished particularly in times of crisis. The need to answer pragmatic questions, or to confirm Western attitudes has always inspired interest. European conceptions of China have rarely reflected Chinese reality, but have first and foremost been the response to European needs. Specific circumstances, such as an actual confrontation, have occasionally provided a different impulse, but to the West, Chinese history has only represented a possible contribution to philosophical interpretations of world history. This remains so whether a study is ostensibly to serve a current need, or merely to furbish an abstruse sinological 'brick' (Herbert Franke). No external influence since Renaissance times can compare with China as a catalytic agent for Europe (and America), either as an example or as a bogy.

HISTORIOGRAPHY AND THE CHINESE HISTORICAL CONSCIOUSNESS

Long before anyone perpetuated their reflections on the past in written form, people living in the heart of the subsequent Chinese empire made written records of memorable contemporary events. The inscriptions they left on bones and bronze vessels can be dated as far back as the thirteenth century BC. They record oracles, sacrifices, investitures and other significant events. The oracle bones were collected even then, and kept in a kind of archives.

There are supposed already to have been scribes in Ch'in, one of the states of which China was later composed, by the middle of the eighth century. They were responsible for recording events at court and compiling genealogies. Probably these records were of mainly ceremonial use, serving as *aides-mémoire* when sacrifices were being made to the ancestors, for instance. But even at this stage they contained, in the chronological, annalistic ordering of their material (*chi*), a formal element characteristic of later Chinese historiography. A parallel development was the writing down of oral traditions (*chuan*). Political bias was already quite common in these records, some states being given prominence, while others were ignored or disparaged. This was the beginning of the practice of writing history as a political corrective, putting a moral interpretation on the past. It is not known when the recording of past events for ritual purposes first became rational interpretation of the past in political and ethical terms. It may have been with the *Book of Documents* (*Shu-ching*), until very recently regarded as the oldest 'history', and one of the earliest examples of this kind of political documentation. It comprises a series of orations, programmatic writings and genealogical tables, allegedly reaching back seventeen hundred years. Parts of the text apparently date from the early Chou period. Others, retaining the style of earlier parts, may have been added in the fourth century BC, to establish further the book's argument, the legitimacy of the Chou dynasty. Such imaginative reconstruction of texts or part of texts believed lost subsequently characterized much writing of Chinese men of letters. Another fundamental trait of the Chinese historiographic tradition originated in the Chou period was the paraphrasing of existing texts, insinuating an idea into a text in order to formulate particular political principles. Disparate historical events were linked together to form a sequence of causes and effects, and historical laws not actually present in the text were allowed to be inferred. Confucius reputedly found the straightforwardly chronological annals of his home state of Lu, known by the title *Spring and Autumn* (*Ch'un-ch'iu*), unsatisfactory as an exposition of the interlocking relationship of heaven, earth and mankind; therefore, it is said, he rewrote them. This example was followed nearly fifteen centuries later by the most prominent of the co-founders of Neo-Confucianism, Chu Hsi, who rewrote Ssu-ma Kuang's *Comprehensive Mirror for Aid in Government* as *Outlines and Details Based on the Comprehensive Mirror*. To the early Confucians the *Spring and Autumn Annals* were less a history book than a textbook of political ethics.

The *Records of the Historian* (*Shih-chi*) of the Han period inaugurated a new kind of historiography. They combined reporting of events with historical fables and 'lore from the past'. This work was started by a court astrologer, Ssu-ma T'an (d. 110 BC), and completed by his son Ssu-ma Ch'ien (145–86? BC). Covering the whole epoch from mythological times to the beginning of the Han period, the tendentious distribution of praise and blame (*pao-pien*) in the book was intended to make it a textbook for the guidance of present and future generations; at the same time, however, it was a vindication of the Han government of the day. The Ssu-ma father and son were like most of the 'historians' of the Chou period, and probably of the Shang period as well, in being also astrologers. The interpretation of the past and of the future were still identical in function. The *Records of the Historian* are made up of several interrelating parts, centring on particular individuals. The first part comprises annals of rulers regarded as belonging to the legitimate tradition; the second part consists of genealogies from the separate states of the Chou period and the royal fiefs of the Early Han period; the third part contains dissertations on subjects of particular political importance, such as religious rites, music, the calendar, irrigation and economics; the fourth part is devoted to the numerous states of the Chou period; the fifth part is a compilation from individual sources, principally biographies, but it also includes accounts of races from the borders of the realm. This arrangement was adopted, with the exception of the fourth part, by Pan Ku (AD 32–92) in the *Book of the [Former] Han Dynasty* (*Han-shu*), with a great expanded topographical section. It also had additional sections on penal legislation, the army, omens, administrative geography and the census. Pan Ku's work became the model for all subsequent dynastic histories. In contrast to Ssu-ma T'an and Ssu-ma Ch'ien, Pan Ku had been officially commissioned to write the previous dynasty's history. The writing of history became an instrument of the state; that is, an institution of the legitimate succession (*cheng-t'ung*).

It was not until the T'ang period, however, that it was literally institutionalized by the setting up of a Historiographical Office (*shih-kuan*). This was attached to the Imperial Secretariat, like the Palace Library; the scribes thus had direct access to all important documents and sources, although that does not mean that they could use them freely. Most of the archival material is lost today, so that for the history of China up to the end of the first millennium AD the dynastic compilations are the most important sources. They are based above all on the *Diaries of Activity and Repose* [of the emperor] (*ch'i-chü chu*),

Records of Current Government (*shih-cheng chi*), *Daily Records* (*jih-li*), *Veritable Records* (Registers) (*shih-lu*), *Biographies* (*lieh-chuan*), *Collected Statutes* (*hui-yao; hui-tien*) and *Dynastic Histories* (*kuo-shih*). The principal function of the Historiographical Office was to establish conclusive and impeccable historical links between dynastic successors and their predecessors. Not infrequently this process involved suppressing, falsifying or glossing over information about the past, and about a new dynasty's antecedents when it was non-Chinese.

The restrictions placed on authorial freedom by the institutionalization of historiography quickly raised a storm of protest. This in turn produced the first systematic critique of history, *Generalities on History* (*Shih-t'ung*) by Liu Chih-chi (661–721), himself a long-standing former member of the staff of the Historiographical Office. Liu's principal criticisms were that it was no longer possible to make responsible personal judgments, to express a personal opinion, to use freely available material or to work without constant interference from superiors. His recommendations included revision of the older dynastic histories to omit or curtail sections on astrology and omens, or at least avoid linking human events with heavenly phenomena. Instead, he proposed more socially, that is, politically, relevant data on individual cities, families and products. Liu's criticism was not directed against the official, normative character of historiography; it was concerned with the historian's attitude to his sources and to objectivity within the power hierarchy of which he formed a part.

The division of history according to dynasties from the Han onwards stimulated the statesman Ssu-ma Kuang (1018–86) to a new attempt at a comprehensive survey of the past. His *Comprehensive Mirror for Aid in Government* (*Tzu-chih t'ung-chien*) – the title was chosen by the emperor – covers the period from 403 BC to AD 959. Ssu-ma Kuang gave reasons for his selection of material, presented in strict chronological order and giving the element of probability its due. The title of his book unambiguously formulated the functional character of historiography, even when only semi-official, for the first time. The philosopher Chu Hsi (1130–1200), as already mentioned, revised Ssu-ma Kuang's work. His *Outlines and Details Based on the Comprehensive Mirror* (*T'ung-chien kang-mu*) offered guidelines intended to be not merely of pragmatic assistance but above all of moral and ethical value.

It was not only historiographical compilations that henceforth became 'guides to bureaucratic practice, written by civil servants for civil servants' (Balazs). The same function also accrued to the *Encyclopaedias* (*lei-shu*), *Collected Statutes* (*hui-yao*) and *Local Gazetteers* (*fang-chih*) that came into existence in the T'ang and Sung periods. These compilations all rest on a markedly historical basis, and all emphasize administration rather than religion, rational rather than irrational processes, concrete facts rather than speculations. They reflect the increasing bureaucratization of China in those centuries. The encyclopedias, which originated in the establishment of state examinations for civil servants, were manuals of theoretical and practical instruction and information for office holders. The *Collected Statutes* were intended for reference. The *Local Gazetteers*, which eventually covered nearly every administrative region in the empire, were intended as manuals of information for administrators posted to areas with which they were not acquainted. These 'indirect history books' are particularly valuable: partly for their information on the knowledge and values of the civil service of any one period, and partly because they contain more original documents, such as memorials, decrees, letters and protocols, than the larger compilations covering the whole empire. Even so, the amount of authentic 'survivals' – material of use to the modern historian not recorded with any historical intent – is relatively small. Collections of documents exist, but these were often compiled according to aesthetic criteria, and are historically valuable only for the sake of their individual components; generally the only archival collections are recent in date.

The Ch'ing period ushered in a new phase in critical historiography, initiated by a few Ming loyalists, whose consternation at the overthrow of the Chinese Ming dynasty led them to castigate the trend away from the former, practical orientation of history writing. They criticized the metaphysical hypostasization of history that had grown up again from the Sung period onwards; indeed, they held it partly responsible for the overthrow of the Ming. The scholar Huang Tsung-hsi (1610–95) advocated 'concrete historical life' and condemned idealistic, intuitive argumentation in the writing of history. Ku Yen-wu (1613–82) demanded practical information from the historian, of use to the state. Wang Fu-chih (1619–92) rejected the Utopian universalism deriving from Neo-Confucianism and demanded a 'national' historiography, by which he ultimately meant 'anti-Manchu'. This criticism was necessarily limited in its expression by the new dynasty's promotion of dogmatic Confucianism. A more prominent feature of the historiography of the early Ch'ing period is its philologically based textual criticism (*k'ao-cheng hsüeh*). By the light of this nearly all the standard texts of Confucianism were examined and subjected to valuable, long overdue correction. The priority given to textual criticism shows clearly that in China, too, philology offered a refuge to historians in times of oppression. Later developments also show, however, that hardly a single idea of the sceptical criticism of the seventeenth century was lost, even though buried in works like those of Wang Fu-chih until the nineteenth century. The path to a national historiography was laid down in advance. The historical and textual criticism of the early Ch'ing period appeared to offer everything necessary for either parrying or absorbing, as desirable, the ideas that flooded into China from the West in the nineteenth century. Thus it was possible, for instance, for K'ang Yu-wei (1858–1927), a spokesman of the reform movement of 1898, to interpret original Confucianism as a revolutionary doctrine, which already adumbrated ideas like the parliamentary system, constitutional monarchy and a professional civil service which the West was now introducing to China. K'ang Yu-wei's interpretation of Confucius was probably not very different from the way Confucius himself had treated early Chou sources: interpreting the historical authority in a way that suited his own political preconceptions. To put it another way: 'Confucianism knew, at bottom, only one form of argument: the historical' (Kemper); expressed by the Chinese as 'drawing on the past to alter [present-day] institutions' (*t'o-ku kai-chih*).

The traditional Chinese historians had great faith, not to say credulity, in their sources. They felt no qualms at sacrificing a significant detail to confirm schematic categories. Quotations and paraphrases from the works of others often took the place of lengthy arguments of their own. They despised 'intuitive' embellishment. There were works guilty of it, designated 'historical tales' (*ku-shih*, *yeh-shih*), in which, as in fiction and drama, the 'objective', dry history of the official and semi-official versions was freely re-created. These works of historicizing literature are as valuable an addition to sources available to the modern historian as the 'brush notes' or notebooks (*pi-chi*), which stand halfway between the official and semi-official histories and the historical tales, and which Lin Yu-t'ang (b. 1895) has described as the 'laziest form of literature', since they display neither formal organization nor inner coherence.

A survey of Chinese historiography cannot close with the disintegration of traditional China. The ensuing discussion itself originated

23

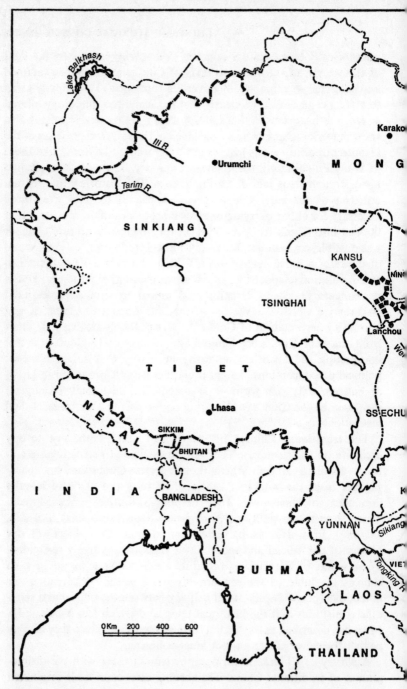

Map of China, showing frontier changes from earliest times to the present day. The symbols used to denote the frontiers in particular periods have

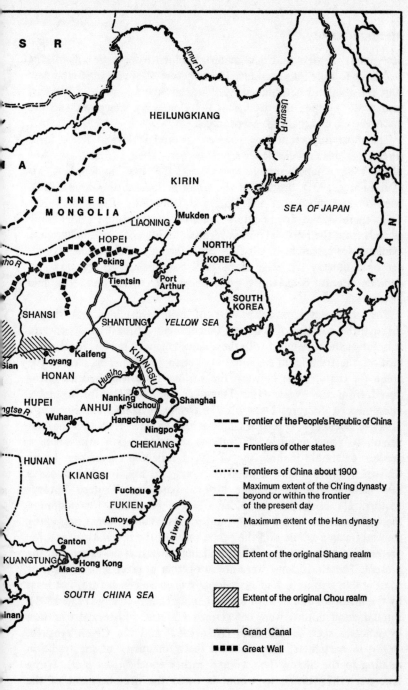

S R

A

HEILUNGKIANG

Amur R.

KIRIN

Ussuri R.

INNER MONGOLIA

LIAONING •Mukden

SEA OF JAPAN

HOPEI

iho R. •Peking

•Tientsin Port Arthur

NORTH KOREA

JAPAN

SHANSI

SHANTUNG YELLOW SEA

SOUTH KOREA

Sian •Loyang •Kaifeng

KIANGSU

Huaiho

HONAN

HUPEI •Wuhan ANHUI Nanking• •Suchou •Shanghai

ngtse R. Hangchou•

•Ningpo

CHEKIANG

HUNAN

KIANGSI

•Fuchou

FUKIEN

•Amoy

Taiwan

•Canton

KUANGTUNG •Hong Kong
•Macao

SOUTH CHINA SEA

inan

- – - – Frontier of the People's Republic of China

- - - - Frontiers of other states

• • • • Frontiers of China about 1900

— · — Maximum extent of the Ch'ing dynasty beyond or within the frontier of the present day

— · · — Maximum extent of the Han dynasty

▨ Extent of the original Shang realm

▨ Extent of the original Chou realm

═══ Grand Canal

▪▪▪▪ Great Wall

been combined where they overlap; hence - · - indicates the frontier both
as it was in about 1900 and as it is under the People's Republic of China.

new points of view and new material, which foreign sino-historians also have to take into account. Three factors above all made the new start possible and determined its character: the adoption of Western historical concepts, the decline of the Confucian viewpoint and the discovery of, or access to, new sources.

The most important new sources are archaeological finds, from several periods: oracle bones from the early period (first finds: An-yang, 1888), paper manuscripts from the first millennium AD (Tun-huang, 1901), bronzes of the Chou period (north China, 1920), bamboo inscriptions of the Han and Chin eras (Etsingol, 1930). Then there is the documentary material of the Ming and Ch'ing periods from the imperial and governmental libraries, gradually made available for research. Finally, the breakthrough of the spoken language as a literary language since 1919 has opened up folk art and demotic literature as sources of, above all, social and economic history.

The dominant Confucian view of history declined not simply through the collapse of a regime that thought of itself as Confucian. It began at the very latest with the abandonment of the last ideological bastion, the traditional examination system, in 1905. This cleared the arena for the struggle between the various historical theories introduced from the West. Hsia Tseng-yu (1882?–1924), for instance, attempted to interpret Darwin's *The Origin of Species* and Spencer's *Study of Sociology* against a Chinese background. Hsia was the first person to reject traditional methods of presentation and wrote a modern textbook, making use of recent Japanese experience. Liang Ch'i-ch'ao (1873–1929), a pupil of K'ang Yu-wei, tried to devise a new methodology of Chinese history, based on Western history-writing. He criticized the older Chinese historians for confining themselves to the court and prominent individuals, while neglecting the empire as a whole and the broad mass of the population, and for preferring facts to ideas, and emphasizing the past at the expense of the present. These criticisms were not altogether unprecedented: they, or comparable opinions, had occasionally been voiced before, not least by the historian and man of letters Chang Hsüeh-ch'eng (1738–1801). Fundamental doubts were entertained about the historical tradition by scholars such as Hu Shih (1891–1962) and Ku Chieh-kang (b. 1895); in particular, they doubted the authenticity of the tradition relating to the Shang dynasty and earlier epochs (*i-ku p'ai*). Wang Kuo-wei (1877–1927), to whom is owed the decipherment of the

24

inscriptions on the oracle bones, was not prepared to accept anything that was not confirmed by archaeological discoveries (*k'ao-ku p'ai*).

Marxist historians introduced new priorities, and concentrated on economic questions and the theory of linear historical development. The theory of progress, in particular, caused the early Marxist historians in China to regard their own history as an exception to the rule. For them, as for Marx himself, China had not changed for two thousand years. The image thus returned to China of a stable society, which Europe had formed on the Chinese model in past centuries, first as an ideal, later as an emblem of a lack of history, and therefore of a lack of progress. The earliest Marxist works revolved around how it had been possible for China not to have experienced any fundamental alterations over so long a period. Authors like Tao Hsi-sheng (b. 1893) and Kuo Mo-jo (b. 1895) found the answer in the fact that feudal elements, represented by the class of civil servants and landowners, continued to dominate society even after the collapse of feudalism in the wake of the Ch'in victory, so that capitalism had not been able to develop. Both these writers also believed that the situation had not changed even after the collapse of the monarchy. Fan Wön-lan (b. 1899) was in fundamental agreement with them as far as the structure of Chinese society, and therefore of Chinese history, was concerned, but differed in his view that the character of Chinese society had changed with the Opium War. Up to the Opium War, Chinese history had been characterized only by the conflict between the peasants and the landowners. Subsequently, however, the struggle against foreign capitalism had been joined to the struggle against the feudalism of the landowners. Up to the first post-war years, the principal theme of the Marxist historians remained the economic and social development of China and the character of Chinese society. As the victory of the Communist movement became steadily more assured, interest grew in the revolutionary past of the Chinese people. Numerous works were published attempting to prove that China had a revolutionary tradition reaching back to the dawn of history. If early Marxists tried to confirm a universal pattern of history in the Chinese past, non-Marxists, even in the twentieth century, not infrequently concluded that Chinese and European history were qualitatively different. Ch'ien Mu (b. 1895), for instance, argues that once overthrown, Western social organizations have never been renewed, whereas Chinese history has been marked by a constant alternation of renewal and decline, of order and chaos. Advancing

25

this as proof of the stability of China, Ch'ien Mu comes, like the Marxists, to a fundamentally optimistic conclusion about the future of China. But not of Europe: Western man, he says, can find no grounds in his own history for a similar confidence that everything will fall into place again.

The increasing polarization of internal political differences from 1927 onwards was echoed by a polarization in historical research and historical writing. This was physically delineated in 1949 when the two rival Chinese states, Nationalist and Communist, took up fixed positions on either side of the Strait of Taiwan. In both parts of China today the historian is once more, in a very special sense, the servant of politics and a focus of political tensions. It is probably no coincidence that the violent attacks on leading historians like Wu Han, Teng T'o, Chien Po-tsan and Hou Wai-lu in 1963 introduced the campaign of rectification that shook the People's Republic of China for several years and led up to the 'Great Proletarian Cultural Revolution'. On Taiwan, too, reputable historians such as Wang Shih-chieh and Kuo T'ing-i have been the objects of violent political criticism from the inception of the 'Cultural Renaissance', planned as a counter-movement to the Cultural Revolution. In the two parts of China the accusations differ. On the mainland the historians mentioned above are charged with bourgeois 'historicism' (*li-shih chu-i*): in deprecating the over-emphasis on the revolutionary character of Chinese popular uprisings in the past, they have compromised the 'revolutionary tradition of the Chinese masses'. On Taiwan the historians are accused of 'conspiring with international Communism', because they have worked closely with liberal American scholars (J. K. Fairbank). The motives underlying the accusations on both sides are comparable, however, and similar to those of past centuries: dissatisfaction on the part of those who hold the political power with the historians' criticism of the present and with their failure to collaborate in research and writing that would serve the current system of government.

Historical writing and historical research are the expressions of historical awareness. The most important characteristic of the traditional Chinese view of history is the awareness of continuance. This is fundamentally different from the traditional European and Occidental historical sense, which conceives of history as a movement in time towards a goal. In ancient China, at least from the end of the Chou period, changes were regarded as deviations from a prescribed, permanent ideal that had been realized in the 'absolute' past. Every

26

new seizure of power was understood to be an attempt to restore the bygone order (*fu-ku*), or at least had to present itself as such. The precept of the fundamental continuity of the world lent the past normative character: since past and present belonged to basically the same dimension, the past could be a source of directly relevant instruction. Herein is rooted the belief that history can provide orientation for current actions. Ch'ien Mu demonstrates that the awareness of continuance is still very much alive: 'It is the Chinese view that the material world and the forms of life in the world can go on developing, but the fundamental principle (*tao*) is the same from beginning to end.' This sense of time is reflected in the old Chinese written language, which does not possess different tenses for past, present and future actions. 'The "line" of time on which, in our way of thinking, "now" is a point continually moving forwards, is [to the Chinese] a "plane" of time, on which the past and the present, and the future as well, merge with each other' (Bauer).

However, traditional China did not regard the state of the world at any given moment as the product of chance. Instead, it was seen as the outcome of the interplay of the three forces, heaven (*t'ien*), earth (*ti*) and man (*jen*), in which man, living between heaven and earth, is subject to a moral imperative that he disregards only at peril of his existence. Sounding out and expounding the tension between nature and man, between past and future, was the task of the priest-scribes (*shih*) of the Shang and Chou periods, and of the historio-graphers (*shih*; the same written character) as well, under the emperors. History was regarded as the accumulation of the whole of human experience, gained through both correct and incorrect behaviour: yet another reason for the particular nature of the traditional Chinese attitude towards history.

That attitude was responsible for a formal peculiarity of Chinese historiography: the repetition of stereotyped formulas to denote values and the passage of time. This creates the impression that nothing new happened, that there was no development, for thousands of years. But this was not their purpose. The real significance of the formula was that in so far as the old thing happened, the right thing happened, or that at least a claim could be made that it was right. It was only in the formulas that the normative quality of history was illuminating and that history gave an assurance that the orientation, the preconceptions, were correct.

It is in this context that the dynastic cycle should be seen; that is, the cyclic approach to and withdrawal from the permanent idea apparently manifest in the course pursued by the separate dynasties. The beginning of each cycle was essentially an 'annulling of time' (Eliade), an affirmation of continuance, in that each dynasty claimed legitimacy through identification with the archetype of the assumption of power, or of the 'mandate of heaven' (*t'ien-ming*), as the Chou called it after the fall of the Shang. The establishment of each new dynasty was understood to be a return to the regular order, the ideal of the Golden Age. Chinese historians have always stressed the personal factor in their interpretation of the allegedly, or actually, cyclic course of history. Founding emperors were for them not merely strong, skilful politicians and generals but also personalities of outstanding moral and ethical qualities. The last rulers of any dynasty, meanwhile, were regarded as degenerate and vicious. The personal factor is not excluded altogether by modern Western historians, either; but they do regard it as but one element among many. The dynastic cycle is generally viewed today as a complex concatenation of causes and effects. Personal, economic and fiscal, administrative and political elements are all seen to work together, creating a supra-economic cycle of conjunct factors. Greatly simplified, in the major dynasties the cycle runs as follows: 1 Seizure of power by a strong leader; relief of social grievances; concentration of revenues; 2 Growth of personal privileges; weakening of the central power; rise in expenditure; fall in revenues; growth of social grievances; 3 Attempts to restore central power; efforts at reform; 4 Accelerating decline of the central power, the administration, the economic and fiscal structure and military security; breakaway of peripheral regions; 5 Struggle for power, rise of a new dynasty.

The cycles, or dynasties, seemed to traditional Chinese the 'natural' units of larger temporal regions, as they were seen standing in an immediate relationship to universal nature. For historiographers in China, the periodization of history was more than a division into genealogical sequences, according to the course of political history. It was a division of all human events from a suprahuman perspective.

THE PERIODIZATION OF CHINESE HISTORY

The connection between concepts of history and periodization makes adoption of the traditional divisions very problematical in non-Chinese writing. Even when such, to outsiders, abstract terms as

28

Han, Ming, Ch'ing are defined more precisely by additional qualifications, such as 'the Sung period: bureaucratic China' or 'the Ming national dynasty: the efflorescence of Mandarin society' (Herbert Franke/Trauzettel), the division still rests on a dynastic foundation, acceptance of which is primarily a matter of outlook. Moreover, the qualifying phrases in the two examples chosen could perfectly well be interchanged: the Sung dynasty was 'national' by contrast with the Chin-Tartars, and the Ming period was also bureaucratic. To the same degree that the dynastic division of history had special significance for the traditional Chinese, it is a positive hindrance to the modern observer from outside China, in his attempts to periodize Chinese history. It has led, on the one hand, to combinations of preceding and main dynasties (Ch'in-Han, Sui-T'ang). On the other hand it has produced subdivisions, such as the practice of splitting the T'ang dynasty into two, with the Late T'ang and the Sung together forming one period, the 'Golden Age of Chinese culture' (Reischauer/Fairbank). As soon as the criteria for division move beyond genealogy, dynastic periodization falls to pieces.

On the other hand, the divisions into ancient, medieval and modern current in European history-writing since the sixteenth or seventeenth century pose equally intractable problems. For one thing they create impressions that are misleading, especially to the European mind, and can be avoided only by additional information: 'the Chinese Middle Ages (AD 200–600)' (Herbert Franke/Trauzettel) has been one suggestion; while for Otto Franke the Chinese Middle Ages last from the Ch'in to the end of the nineteenth century. For another thing, it is hard to describe characteristics that would make the three epochs equally applicable to every historical continuum. For instance, Chinese history has no Dark Ages. Other periodizations of universal history, naturally including China, have been suggested: Karl Jaspers' 'axial period' (800–200 BC), and the recurrent 'epochal types' of Spengler, Toynbee and Sorokin, among others. H. O. Stange has taken China as the basis of a periodization for which he claims universal validity, at least in respect of continental Asia, Europe and North Africa. It is based on two 'world-shaking events': the 'inundation' of East and West by mounted races from central Asia, and the 'revolutionary upheavals' resulting from Western expansionism. None of these suggested systems has had any decisive effect as yet on modern periodization of Chinese history.

Only in the Socialist states has extensive consensus been reached on periodization, covering Chinese history as well, based on the Marx-Engels programme of mankind's development. Even so no general agreement exists on the dates of each stage: there are disparities of a thousand years or more. Frequently Soviet Sino-historians, and sometimes the Chinese too, apply the traditional epochal divisions to China, alongside the Marx-Engels stages (Soviet Academy of Sciences: *Synology*, 1967). According to these, Chinese antiquity ends with the Han, the Middle Ages with the seventeenth century and the 'modern' era with the twentieth, before the start of 'contemporary history'. Among Chinese Marxists, however, there is some disputing these divisions. Their primary concern is to demonstrate in Chinese history the stages of development that are derived essentially from the European example. The main problem here is definition: how long was China a slave-owning society? (only in the Shang period, or in the Western Chou period as well?); how long did feudalism last? (2,000 or 2,500 years?); when were the 'seeds' of capitalism sown? (Sung period? Ming period?); when did the modern period begin? (general agreement here: the Opium War).

Criteria of European origin are equally characteristic of the attempts at periodization made by most modern Japanese Sino-historians. Typically, though, they prefer divisions according to particular phenomena (intellectual or material culture, social order, ethnogenesis, the shifting pattern of inter-state relationships). Naka Michiyo (1851–1908), for example, writing at a time when Chinese history was still hidebound by the traditional formulas, divided it into three periods, each of three dynasties. These were: Hsia, Shang, Chou – antiquity, times of cultural initiative; Han, T'ang, Sung – Middle Ages, time of cultural entrenchment and continuation without formal renewal; Yüan, Ming, Ch'ing – modern age, time of cultural refinement and decline. Kuwabara Jitsuzō (1871–1931) distinguished the following periods: antiquity (to the end of the Chou dynasty) – expansion of the Chinese race; Middle Ages (to the end of the T'ang) – hegemony of the Chinese race; late Middle Ages (to the end of the Ming) – heyday of the Mongols; modern age (to the early twentieth century) – encroachment of Europeans. Naitō Torajiro (1866–1934) devised a scheme which has been more widely accepted than either of those – and among Western historians too, particularly on account of his demarcation of the modern era. His view corresponded more obviously with the 'universal' history of the Far East, and his divisions are as follows: antiquity (to the middle of the Later Han) – development

30

and expansion of Chinese culture; first transitional period (second half of the Later Han to the Western Chin) – halt in the spread of Chinese culture among the races on its borders; Middle Ages (to the middle of the T'ang) – centripetal reaction from the now stronger neighbouring peoples; second transitional period (to the Period of the Five Dynasties) – culmination of China's external influence; modern age (Sung to Ch'ing) – renewed external expansion by China, but also reciprocal encroachment by the outside world and a balance of coexistence.

Many more examples could be given, but it must be clear already that the dynastic periodization of Chinese history, if anything, creates more problems than it solves. Every system of subdividing history, including that of China, must be functional if it is to claim more than 'merely mnemotechnical interest' (Croce).

2 Geography

The physical characteristics of an area in which a social formation evolves are not fixed, once and for all. Instead, they are in part drawn into the process of social evolution. Chinese history is a significant example of the effect on Nature of human interference, perhaps provoked by Nature itself in the first place. It also shows how Nature, so affected, subsequently affects the course of history. The repeated attempts to regulate the flow of the Huangho and their influence on subsequent events give Herder's dictum that 'history is geography in motion' a more literal meaning than he can have intended. Geographical circumstances are not immutable historical factors – as has often been asserted with reference to the alleged 'insularity' of the 'Middle Kingdom' (Schwind). The delimiting effect of physical frontiers is generally less than might be supposed. Human attitudes and actions are indeed affected, of course. But such influence is relative and dependent on the stage of development of the social formation in question. Physical characteristics can be changed or overcome and their nature as historical factors thereby transformed. The evolution of the area settled and ruled by the Chinese demonstrates that historical regions are not necessarily identical with geographical ones.

PHYSICAL CHARACTER OF THE HISTORICAL REGION

A synoptic geographical survey of the historical region of China must take it in at its maximal extent, that is, at a moment in history when the geographical conditions, too, will not necessarily be identical to earlier moments. Three illustrations will suffice. So far, in historical times, the Huangho has substantially altered its lower course six times. Each of these changes was of the same order of magnitude as a diversion of the mouth of the Rhine from Rotterdam to Danzig.

32

The region to the south of the middle and lower Yangtse is regarded today as a centre of rice-growing on a large scale. It is a totally cultivated region where hardly a trace remains of its original state. Yet as late as the Chou dynasty, little more than two thousand years ago, the greater part of the region was covered with sub-tropical swamps, inhabited by elephants and giant lizards. Forest clearance is believed today to have played a part comparable to that of natural erosion in changing the topography of the central Chinese loess regions (Shansi, Shensi). The forests that originally spread over the high plateau of the loess region have been almost entirely cut down in the last two thousand years. The chains of hills are mostly bare today, but were probably still generously wooded as recently as the Han dynasty. The loss of the original vegetation has damaged both the water table and the structure of the surface. The Chinese were far from regarding these changes as undesirable interference with Nature. One of their legendary heroes, Yü the Great, owed his undying fame to his construction of roads and canals and his forest clearance, whereby he changed the face of the realm in the space of thirteen years.

Orographically, however, the terrain of China has remained virtually unchanged throughout the country's recorded history. Taking the broad view, there is obviously an extraordinary variety in the area bordered by the Pamir, Tienshan and Altai ranges in the west, the Sea of Japan and the China Seas to the east, the Himalayas and connected ranges to the south and the Siberian plains to the north. Almost every type of landscape and climate are to be met with in this immense area, from the sub-tropical conditions of the coast, part of which is even tropical and lies within the hurricane zone, to the sub-polar continental tundra, and from the humid fluvial plains in the temperate zone, to the arid and semi-arid deserts and mountains. The one outstanding characteristic, amid all this variety, is mountainousness. Well over half the country's area is more than 3,000 feet above sea level; only about 10 per cent lies below 1,600 feet. It is above all mountains, and not rivers, that break up the area. The several different systems, running from west to east and from north to south, have created significant subdivisions.

In very close proximity to the geographical centre, the Kunlun range stretches eastwards from the Pamirs, reaching heights of over 20,000 feet. It branches into the Chinling range, which also rises in places to 13,000 feet, the Huaiyang mountains and the Tapieh mountains, which reach far into the centre of China and form the dividing line between north and south. The other east–west chain is made up of the Karakorum mountains and the Himalayas, and the adjoining Hengtuan range branching off to the south. In the north the Tienshan, Altai, Tannu, Sayan, Yablonovy and Lesser Hsingan ranges follow one after the other, building a frontier wall of varying heights.

In eastern China there are two sequences from north to south, one following the coastline, the other the Great East Asian Fold. Both start from the central grid of mountains in south China. The more easterly runs along the coastal mountains of the south-east, culminating in the Wuyi range, and continues via the highlands of Shantung, and the Changpai range between Korea and Manchuria to the Sichota–Alin range on the north-east coast. The more westerly range is higher and more continuous. It consists of the Wuling range, the Taihang mountains and the Greater Hsingan. The ranges aligned from north to south in the central Asian area do not form a coherent system. The Pamir, Altyn Tagh, the Mongolian Altai and Changai ranges may be mentioned.

Within this network of mountains there are two major climatic frontiers of essentially orographic foundation. They divide the historical region of China into three great productive regions, differing in their topography and scenery as they have differed in their culture and population at various times and in varying degrees. The first of these frontiers, the latitudinal division between the two main temperature zones, is formed by the Chinling range and its spurs. To the north of it the soil is predominantly loess. The cold winters permit only one harvest a year over most of the area. The severity of the winters increases rapidly towards the north and north-west and there are corresponding decreases in rainfall and the length of the growing season. The crops that do best in the area are those typical of the temperate zone (cereals). This is the area originally settled by the 'Chinese' people of early historical times. The soil to the south of the temperature frontier is mostly red: alluvial deposits and sandstone. Agriculture is dominated by rice-growing in submerged paddy-fields. The climate is predominantly sub-tropical – humid and warm. Several harvests are possible each year; the growing season lasts from nine to twelve months; sub-tropical crops do best. The original inhabitants of this region were mainly Thai.

In the north, with its cold dry winters, the only major crop originally was probably the indigenous millet. In the second millennium BC

34

and later, multirowed barley arrived from Tibet and sorghum millet (*kaoliang*) and wheat from western Asia. Wheat is today the most widespread single crop. Millet remains the principal crop in the peripheral regions of the west and north-west, where drought is a constant threat. Rice was probably already known in the Chinese heartland in the north in the second millennium BC, but it was only with the mass colonization of the greater Yangtse area by the Chinese (after the Han period) that it became the staple crop of China. Since then rice and wheat cultivation have overlapped, especially in the intermediate zone between north and south. Nowadays rice is grown wherever the necessary conditions exist or can be artificially created. Wheat is grown in the south above all as a subsidiary crop. Both crops drop off rapidly towards the north, in the case of rice, and south, in the case of wheat.

The second major climatic frontier is meridional, running along the Greater Hsingan, the highlands in the region of the great arc of the Huangho, the eastern flanks of the Kunlun range and the Hengtuan mountains. It separates the zone where rainfall makes arable farming possible from the arid and semi-arid steppes and deserts. The land to the east of this line is the area of specifically 'Chinese' settlement and occupancy: 'Inner China', the 'Eighteen Provinces' of the later empire. To the west of the line crop growing is only possible in the oases on the fringes of the mountains. Extensive areas of the high plateau, especially in Mongolia and Tibet, however, can be used for grazing.

There are nineteen different topographical areas that can be distinguished in greater detail. Considerable local variations are to be found within each of them, but in their general characteristics each displays a high degree of uniformity.

Plains

MANCHURIAN PLAIN (central Manchuria): extremely cold, dry winters; humid, warm summers; even rainfall; growing season 150–180 days; forested steppe region; summer wheat, soya beans, sorghum millet.

NORTH CHINESE PLAIN (Hopei, Honan, northern Anhui, western Shantung): cold winters; humid, hot summers; high annual variations in rainfall; growing season 180–240 days; temperate/warm-zone vegetation; winter wheat, soya beans, sorghum millet.

LOWER YANGTSE PLAIN (southern Anhui, Kiangsu, northern Chekiang): humid, warm year-round temperature; high, even rainfall;

growing season 240–270 days; warm/humid-zone vegetation; rice, winter wheat.

MIDDLE YANGTSE PLAIN (southern Anhui, northern Kiangsi, Hupei, northern Hunan): humid, warm year-round temperature; high, even rainfall; growing season 300–360 days; warm/humid-zone vegetation; rice, winter wheat.

PEARL RIVER PLAIN (southern Kuangtung): humid, year-round heat; high, even rainfall; growing season 360 days; tropical vegetation; rice.

Hill Country

SOUTH MANCHURIAN HIGHLANDS (southern Manchuria): cold winters, warm summers; even rainfall; growing season 150 days; dry/cold-zone vegetation; summer wheat, sorghum millet.

SHANTUNG HIGHLANDS (eastern Shantung): cold winters, warm summers; moderate, even rainfall; growing season 180–210 days; temperate/warm-zone vegetation; winter wheat, sorghum, soya beans.

SOUTH-EAST COASTAL HIGHLANDS (southern Chekiang, Fukien, eastern Kuangtung): humid, hot; high, even rainfall; growing season 300–360 days; tropical/sub-tropical vegetation; rice, taro.

SOUTH CHINA HIGHLANDS (Kuangsi, southern Hunan, southern Kiangsi, northern Kuangtung): humid, warm; moderate, even rainfall; growing season 180–210 days; humid/warm-zone vegetation; rice, taro.

River Basins

SHENSI BASIN (Shensi): cold winters, warm, humid summers; high annual variations in rainfall; growing season up to 200 days; tempate/warm-zone vegetation; winter wheat, millet.

KANSU BASIN (Kansu): cold winters, warm summers; extremely high annual variations in rainfall; growing season 175–200 days; temperate warm-zone vegetation; millet, summer wheat.

SSECHUAN BASIN (Ssechuan): humid, hot; high, even rainfall; growing season 300–360 days; humid/warm-zone vegetation; rice, winter wheat.

TSAIDAM BASIN (Tsinghai): desert.

DSUNGARIAN BASIN (northern Sinkiang): wide temperature range annually; cool summers; low, even rainfall; growing season 115–140 days (in oases at the foot of the mountains); grazing land, steppe; summer wheat.

36

TARIM BASIN (southern Sinkiang): extremely wide temperature range annually; hot summers; extremely low rainfall; growing season 175–200 days (in oases at the foot of the mountains); desert; winter wheat.

Plateaux

SHANSI PLATEAU (Shansi): cold winters, warm summers; high variations annually in rainfall; growing season up to 180 days; temperate/ warm-zone vegetation; winter wheat, millet.

SOUTH-WESTERN PLATEAU (Yünnan, Kueichou): mild winters, warm summers; high, even rainfall; growing season 270–300 days; humid/ warm-zone vegetation; rice, winter wheat.

MONGOLIAN PLATEAU (Mongolia): wide temperature range annually; warm summers; winters extremely dry; low, and in places very uneven, rainfall; growing season 90–100 days; grazing steppe.

TIBETAN PLATEAU (Tibet): cold to extremely cold; low, uneven rainfall; growing season 140–150 days (in river oases); grazing steppe, desert; barley.

It remains to mention the great river systems, which have a decisive effect on the character of the terrain, though they do not subdivide it. The most important ones all flow eastwards: the Amur–Ussuri group, the Huangho–Huaiho group, the Yangtse system and the Pearl River–Sikiang group. The constant threat that the last four hundred or more miles of the Huangho's course represent to the North Chinese plain has already been mentioned. With the passage of time the river has deposited so much soil along its course that its bed is six feet higher on average than the level of the surrounding plains. Tributaries are only able to enter it as it flows through the Shantung highlands. The excessive amounts of mud it carries along, the alluvial cone it forms and its continual variations of course, are all part of the river's danger for the plains. As smaller rivers and streams can neither flow into it nor reach the sea, because the fall of the land is so slight, their water accumulates in swamps and marshy lakes. The Huaiho is the largest and most dangerous of these stretches of water with limited drainage. Unlike the Huangho, the Yangtse, China's largest river, with the longest course and carrying the greatest volume of water, drains most of the regions that border it. Beside the watercourses of the Red Basin of Ssechuan, its principal tributaries along the

37

twelve hundred miles of its lower reaches are two natural reservoirs, Tungtinghu (Hunan) and Poyanghu (Kiangsi), in the middle Yangtse plain.

Some mention of the variations of the Chinese coastline is apposite here. With the exception of the hilly Liaotung and Shantung peninsulas, the whole of the coastal region north of the Yangtse is a flat alluvial plain, with a smooth outline. South of the Yangtse, the steeply sloping terrain is riddled with creeks and inlets, that in places cut deep inland. The northern part, especially from the Yangtse to Shantung, has the reputation of inaccessibility: the 'iron' coast. It is this that provokes frequent references to China's 'remoteness from the sea'. Here, for the Chinese, the sea 'was merely the cessation of the land' (Hegel). On the south coast, on the other hand, there is a visible continuation of the mainland in the form of some 3,500 islands. Of these, 2,900, amounting to 90 per cent of the total island area, lie off the coasts of Chekiang, Fukien and Kuangtung. This section of the coast has played a major role in China's maritime history.

HISTORICAL EXPANSION OF THE CHINESE EMPIRE

The oldest historical region of China is the 'Central Plains' (*Chung-yüan*), those parts of the modern provinces of Honan, Hopei and Shansi which border the middle course of the Huangho and are liable to be flooded by the river. This was the domain of the Shang kings, and later the 'Middle Kingdoms' (*Chung-kuo*: a name used nowadays of China as a whole) of the Chou period. The region lying above the Central Plains, on the west side of the highlands enclosing the North Chinese plain, is equally old historically, or at least not substantially younger. The Shensi basin which, with its subsidiary arms, the valleys of the Fen, Wei, Lo and Ching rivers, encircles the eastern bend of the Huangho, was the domain of the Chou dynasty, before they overthrew the Shang. Being surrounded on all sides by mountains and accessible by way of only four passes, this area was later called 'the land within the passes' (*Kuan-chung*). A specific affinity, as well as tension, existed between these two nuclear regions until well into the second millennium AD. As alluvial land with a high proportion of loess deposits they had geographically much in common. Rival powers arose repeatedly in both regions, whose relationships with each other were generally tense. This tension is already perceptible in the Shang period, when the Chou, who had at first been subject to the Shang in certain respects, successfully rose against their overlords. At this period on both sides of the mountain range the political and economic nuclei were probably identical. The area of external warfare, too, probably did not stretch far from the political and economic nucleus.

This congruence was gradually dissipated during the Chou period. The reason for this was not so much the conquest by King Wu (traditionally 1169–1116 BC) of the greater part of the North Chinese plain and his creation of a relatively loose alliance out of the individual regions; rather it was the economic and political expansion of the individual states. Possibly, in the main the Chou dynasty fell because of their failure to reconcile the tensions between the inner and outer parts of their territories, as defined by economic, political and military factors. Until their expulsion in 772 BC, Chou rule remained most firmly established in their homeland within the passes. After moving their capital to Lo-i (modern Loyang, Honan), they were confined within the Middle Kingdoms, which could expand no further. The peripheral states (Chin, Ch'i), meanwhile, grew stronger, partly through expansion and partly by overcoming the associated problems of administration and communication. At the same period there were 'barbarian' states also growing in strength on the periphery (Yen in the north; Ch'u between the Huai and the Yangtse; Wu and Yüeh on the coast to the north and south of the mouth of the Yangtse). These sought a rapprochement with the Middle Kingdoms, at least up to the middle of the first millennium BC. In particular, they drew up genealogies in support of their claims to a part in the civilization of the inner kingdoms. In the sixth century BC the alliance of states from which imperial China was to grow covered the whole of the region bounded in the north by the line later traced by the Great Wall, in the south by the Yangtse, in the east by the ocean and in the west by the foothills of the Shensi basin.

In the last years of the Chou dynasty, Ch'in and Ch'u were the two border states who made the greatest territorial gains. Ch'u gradually pushed its borders across the Yangtse into the valleys of the modern provinces of Kiangsi and Hunan, driving the original inhabitants into the higher ground to the south. Ch'in, meanwhile, was forced again and again to confront its nomadic neighbours in the north and west. As a result of these confrontations, Ch'in's conquests extended to the vicinity of the modern town of Lanchou (Kansu) by the end of the fourth century BC. At the same time it reached out into the valleys of modern Ssechuan, where two semi-sinized states, Shu and Pa, had grown up. Ch'u, too, enlarged itself at the expense of two semi-sinized border states, Wu and Yüeh.

Very broadly speaking these acts of territorial expansion took place on fronts parallel to the existing borders, rounding off and filling corners. In fact, however, most thrusts were linear, following the traditional lines of communication, especially along valleys; they spread out to take in wide areas only when the existence of plains made it easy. The same principle applied, only on a larger scale, in the offensive and defensive military campaigns that followed immediately on the first unification of the empire under the Ch'in. Under the first Ch'in emperor, Ch'in Shih-huang-ti (259–210 BC), the nomadic Hsiung-nu (Asiatic Huns), who were just starting to organize themselves politically, were driven north out of the arc of the Huangho. The separate northern states had had their own defensive walls, and these were joined up by order of the new overlord to protect his northern frontier. The result was the first continuous rampart, visible over a wide area and marking off the northern limit of the empire. It was also the first time that an ecological frontier was crossed on a wide front. The inclusion of the Ordos desert was the beginning of the strategic advances into non-agrarian areas. Advances of this kind became typical of the Chinese state. Ch'in armies also forced their way across the watersheds in the south of modern Kiangsi and Hunan to the sea, in the vicinity of what was later the city of Canton. This was China's first bridgehead on the South China Sea. It is interesting to note that the early Ch'in rulers were the first to equip maritime expeditions. Ostensibly the fleets were supposed to look for the 'Islands of the Blessed Genii', which were believed to lie in the sea to the north. It is not certain whether the expeditions were motivated by mysticism and magic or by power politics. A combination of both factors is feasible.

Later expansion nearly always took the form of explosive thrusts outwards from the centre, in directions dictated by the orographic systems, reaching as far as was militarily possible. They were characteristic of the reigns of strong emperors, especially the founders of new dynasties. Their motives and intentions were not always defensive, there is evidence that some Chinese emperors had an 'Alexander complex', and felt the need 'to be forever conquering new worlds' (Reischauer). Colonization was in most cases the result of conquest, relatively rarely the purpose. Often it took place only very slowly, over the course of centuries, in areas lying between the paths of separate thrusts. In the meantime it could happen that the radial outcrops of Chinese expansionism crumbled again.

The next more than usually martial emperor after the first of the Ch'in, Han Wu-ti (reigned 141–87 BC), for instance, had to reconquer the avenue first driven to the south by the Ch'in. He also established a second chain of garrisons along a section of the south coast. In 111 BC the Han armies overcame the resistance of the strongest state on the empire's south flank, in the region now covered by Kuangtung and Kuangsi, and along the Tongking delta: the Yüeh (Vietnamese: Viet). This people, who had been driven from the region of the mouth of the Yangtse a few centuries earlier, either had to submit to Han overlordship or migrate yet farther south. The old territories in the Ordos region also had to be reconquered. In the course of these confrontations, however, the Han armies pushed far beyond the limits reached by the Ch'in. These expansionist thrusts, usually described as flanking defensive measures, went deep into central Asia along the chain of oases. Han forces entrenched themselves along the southern edge of the Gobi desert (127–119 BC) and reached as far as the west side of the Pamirs (104–102 BC). In the same period other contingents subdued the semi-sinized state of Chosŏn, an area now partly in southern Manchuria and partly in North Korea (108 BC). Strategic resettlement was undertaken on a large scale for the first time under Han Wu-ti, with the object of filling and securing a particular newly conquered area. Approximately 700,000 Chinese colonists are supposed to have been sent to settle what is now the Kansu Corridor. Han Wu-ti also dispatched expeditions out into the northern seas, though with as little results in the form of territorial gains as those of the Ch'in period. The large island of Hainan in the South China Sea was the only offshore acquisition, and that temporarily. The farthest extremities of the thrusts made by Han Wu-ti already touched the periphery of the area that the Chinese empire was one day to occupy.

The peripheral conquests only achieved enduring significance, however, if they established territorial claims in the historical consciousness which survived, sometimes for centuries, even when the area settled and governed by the Han Chinese was confined to a small nucleus. With the internal decline of the empire from the fourth century AD, the Chinese outposts in central and northern Asia also fell back. Large areas of north China itself came under the rule of nomadic and semi-nomadic mounted tribes. The Chinese nucleus drew back finally into nothing more than the region of the lower

41

Yangtse. Many inhabitants of the north fled southwards from the advancing 'barbarians'. The remaining original inhabitants were driven yet farther. Consequently for the first time Han Chinese occupied the land to the south of the Yangtse in large numbers. The island of Hainan came under Chinese rule for good.

After the Sui had re-united the empire towards the end of the sixth century, the peripheral regions once more attracted the attention of the central power. Sui troops penetrated the Tongking delta for a second time, and made a brief foray into the south-east Asian state of Champa, in the Mekong delta (605). Two seaborne expeditions were launched to 'Liu-ch'iu' (probably Taiwan) (607, 610). In central Asia the Sui managed briefly to subdue part of the Turk race of T'u-chüeh (581) and some of the Mongol-Tibetan tribes in what is now northern Tibet. But all their successes were extremely short-lived, and some of their expeditions, such as those to Taiwan and Champa and the attempts to conquer the Korean kingdom of Koguryō (612–14), were both abortive and catastrophic. Extensive military campaigns in remote regions were not the least of the reasons for the collapse of the Sui dynasty.

Not until the reigns of the T'ang emperors T'ai-tsung (reigned 626–49) and Kao-tsung (reigned 649–83) was it possible to reassemble the dismembered parts of the empire. At that time nearly every corner that Han armies had reached was considered former 'imperial territory'. In three major campaigns (630, 639–40, 647–48) T'ai-tsung's forces, supported by the central Asian Uigurs, conquered the eastern and western branches of the T'u-chüeh, the eastern branch of whom had advanced as far as the upper valleys of the Oxus and Indus on the western side of the Pamirs. For the first time, too, Tibet was drawn into the peripheral field of influence of a Chinese dynasty. T'ai-tsung had no success in Korea; but his successor Kao-tsung managed to break the concerted resistance of Koguryō, Paekche (south-west Korea) and Japanese units. In this enterprise the T'ang were supported by the largest of the three Korean states, Silla, which subsequently united Korea for the first time under its rule (668). Like the central Asian Uigur state, occupying what are now Inner and Outer Mongolia, Silla was not under direct Chinese overlordship, but there were close ties between them. The T'ang set up special military protectorates around the territory under direct Chinese rule, for the security of regions remote from the centre of power and only semi-colonized. These regions were given names reminiscent of the later Russian bastion of Vladivostok ('Govern the East'): 'Pacify the East' (An-tung, in what was later southern Manchuria), 'Pacify the North' (An-pei, in what is now Mongolia), 'Pacify the West' (An-hsi, in the Tarim basin), 'Pacify the South' (An-nan, Annam, in the Tongking delta).

It proved as impossible to maintain for long this overextended empire as it had been for previous dynasties. The need to keep up the appearances of power was irreconcilable with the sparseness of the Chinese population in the south; the garrisons were isolated, the available forces spread too thinly over the ground. From the middle of the eighth century the expanse which had been subdued with such effort began to cave in. In 751 Chinese armies were defeated at Talas in the extreme west, by the advance guard of the forces of Islam as they pushed eastwards; in the same year Chinese detachments were beaten by units from the semi-sinized, but independent Thai state of Nan-chao in the south-west (modern Yünnan).

With the decline of the T'ang and the emergence of a whole series of rival pretenders to the throne, more was lost than the remote, border regions. Large areas of the Chinese heartland, especially in the north, fell into the hands of foreign tribes. The greatest advances were made by the semi-nomadic Kitan, who had already extended their sway from southern Manchuria deep into Mongolia by the beginning of the tenth century. From 946 onwards they were settled in the neighbourhood of the later city of Peking, where they took the Chinese dynastic name of Liao, thereby laying claim to the imperial throne. The Sung rulers, who attempted to re-unite the empire in the middle of the tenth century, were unsuccessful in removing this challenge. Neither were they able to destroy the new, non-Chinese states in the areas of central Asia and Annam formerly conquered by the Han and the T'ang. In the north-west, Tangut Tibetans had founded a strong state with the Chinese name of Hsi-Hsia in and to the west of the Ordos region. In the south, descendants of the Yüeh had once again established an independent state in the Tongking delta. Thus the Sung realm was smaller than that of the other great dynasties, the Han and the T'ang. It could, however, be regarded as an ideal size, for it was a relatively well-rounded entity, a settled economic region, without peripheral projections, of which the Sung were able to keep control for over a century. Then, at the beginning of the twelfth century another northern race of shepherds and hunters, the Jurchen, came rapidly to the fore. A year after successfully rising against the Liao-Kitan, to whom they paid tribute, they took the Chinese dynastic name of Chin (1115). Before the end of the next decade they had driven the Sung out of north China altogether (1125–27). From then onwards the Sung lands reached only as far as the line from the Huai to the Wei. The Chin boundary ran through the modern provinces of Kiangsu, Anhui, Honan and Shensi.

These territorial changes raise the question of whether they reduced China to two-thirds of the extent of its original nucleus. The answer depends on the definition of 'China'. If 'China' means only a region ruled by an ethnic Chinese prince, then China, under the Southern Sung, reached only as far as the Huai and Wei rivers. But in that case China would have ceased to exist under the Mongols and the Manchu emperors, who ruled the whole empire. Such interpretation is inappropriate to administrative, social, economic and cultural realities in times of foreign domination. Above all, this interpretation would be contrary to the view that the Chinese themselves had of their history and of their territory. Dynastic histories were written for nearly all the 'Chinese' dynasties, whether they ruled over the whole or only part of the Chinese heartland. In this way they became part of the historical tradition. The decisive criterion for inclusion in the tradition was whether the area ruled by a foreign dynasty was felt, when seized, to be part of the Chinese heartland. The territorial *nomos* held good for the historical, and therefore also for the political, consciousness in China even throughout centuries of foreign rule. Unlike Western tradition, empire was not defined by the extent of the ruler's territorial possessions. Instead, it defined itself by the function of its administration.

Just as the Liao-Kitan had been defeated by the Chin-Jurchen, the latter were overthrown at the beginning of the thirteenth century by the Mongols, united under the leadership of Jenghis Khan (1155?–1227). At the time of his death almost the whole of the region of central and northern Asia bordering the Chinese heartland lay under Mongol rule. But it was only towards the end of the century that his grandson, Kublai Khan (1215–94), managed to bring China itself under his control. In the course of this conquest, in 1253, the Mongols overran Nan-chao, until then an independent kingdom. Consequently this region, the modern province of Yünnan, was from that time on an integral part of the Chinese state. A large part of the Thai population of Nan-chao migrated to the south and founded the Siamese-Thai nation. The Mongols also made numerous attacks on Burma, Annam, Java and Japan, but without success. Another attempt to conquer the island of Liu-ch'iu (Taiwan) was also ineffectual. Only the small archipelago of the Pescadores was added to the empire, for the first time, towards the end of the Yüan dynasty.

After the Mongols had been driven out of China, the Ming emperors in turn made repeated onslaughts on Mongolian territory. These campaigns, and similar offensives in Manchuria and Annam, restored Chinese dominance for a few decades in the nearer border regions. In the long run, however, they brought no permanent territorial advantages. There were no expansionist thrusts westwards into the heart of the continent, as under the Han and T'ang dynasties. The Ming did send expeditions by sea to western parts of Asia, but no territorial expansion came of it. The Ming empire was not much larger than that of the Northern Sung; it coincided exactly with that region of eastern Asia that by then had been settled by an over-whelmingly Chinese population.

The last permanent addition to China was once more made by a foreign dynasty. Again it led to incongruity between the political, the economic and the settled areas. It was characteristic of the second millennium AD, that foreign rulers were more expansionist than Chinese dynasties in their ambitions. A whole series of reasons can account for it: the foreigners' own peripheral origins, their ethnic or cultural affinities with other races beyond the borders, political concepts beyond the idea of coinciding national and demographic boundaries, and military mobility equal to anything from central Asia.

Like the Mongols four centuries before, some of the tribal chieftains of the Tungusic Jurchen in Manchuria, which had already produced the Chin-Tartars, by banding together, quickly created a powerful force on the Chinese periphery. Their first expansionist thrusts were directed against Korea (1627, 1636–37) and Inner Mongolia (1634–35). In the same period they were already venturing inside the Great Wall. By the end of the seventeenth century they had eliminated the last Chinese pretender to the throne and had the whole of China under their own rule. Territorially, these conquests signified less than the peripheral additions that the Manchu made to 'China'; for China in the twentieth century has laid claim to the full extent of the Manchu empire, not just to the Chinese nuclear heartland ruled over by the ethnic national dynasties of the Sung and the Ming.

The outcome of the Korean campaigns was that the Yi dynasty there entered into a relationship of direct vassalage with the Manchu.

45

This was not relaxed to any extent until the eighteenth century. The Mongolian campaigns had brought some of the East Mongolians under Manchurian rule. Even before their conquest of China the Manchu had already set up a special office to administer the dependencies (*li-fan yüan*) (1638). The Manchu did not remain without rivals in central Asia. Towards the end of the seventeenth century the new masters of China were challenged by the rise of a West Mongol tribe, the Dsungars, who first took the oases in the Tarim basin and then advanced into eastern Mongolia until they threatened Peking itself from the north. The Manchu succeeded in wiping out the West Mongol army in a battle at Urga on the Kerulen River in 1696. Outer Mongolia and the Tarim basin were thus brought back under the direct rule of the emperor in Peking for the first time in nearly a thousand years. Even so the Dsungars, from their principal settlements on the upper reaches of the Ili River, continued to menace the borders of the Manchu empire, until Manchu forces advanced right into Ili and destroyed their last strongholds (1755–57). With that the Chinese empire was extended as far as Lake Balkhash. A military governor was appointed to administer the 'New Frontier March' (Hsin-chiang: Sinkiang). During the Ming period numerous Mongolian tribes had been converted by a new wave of Lamaism. The Dsungars felt particularly close ties with the centre of Lamaism in Tibet and exercised a kind of protective overlordship in Tibet for a time. For strategic reasons, therefore, the Manchu soon turned their attention to the Mongols' spiritual centre. In 1720 Sino-Manchurian forces advanced temporarily as far as Lhasa and the eastern part of Tibet was annexed to Ssechuan. However, the Manchu had to intervene twice more in Tibet (1727–28, 1750), before the entire plateau became nominally part of the Ch'ing empire. The regions bordering the Amur and along the North Pacific coast had already been conquered by the Manchu at an early stage on their road to empire, and Taiwan had fallen to them while they were still dealing with the opposition of Ming loyalists in the south (1683).

China reached its maximum extent under the Manchu regime. It embraced the vast, sparsely populated areas in the north and west as well as all the offshore islands. The spatial expanse went far beyond any notional identification of the state with the demographic entity. The incongruence persists in the twentieth century. China is still engaged in growing into the frontiers laid down by the Manchu.

This extended empire was not threatened again until the nineteenth century; and not by traditional enemies, but by the Western powers and Japan. In 1842 China had to cede Hong Kong to Great Britain; the region north of the Amur and the maritime provinces on the North Pacific were lost to Russia in 1860; the territory around the Ili River and Lake Balkhash also went to Russia (1854, 1871), as did Port Arthur (1898); Germany 'acquired' Kiaochow (1898), and France Kuangchouwan (1898); in 1895 China had to give up Taiwan to Japan. The territorial losses were insignificant compared to the influence which the imperialist powers wielded in the last years of the nineteenth century. If the spheres of influence had become outright colonies, the resulting division might well have destroyed China. It was prevented by rivalry between the great powers and by the developments in the world political situation and in China herself in the twentieth century. In and about the year 1900, however, China was divided into the following spheres of influence:

Russia: Sinkiang, Mongolia, Manchuria.

Germany: Shantung.

Great Britain: Tibet, Ssechuan, Kueichou, Hupei, Hunan, Honan, Anhui, Kiangsi, Kiangsu, Chekiang, eastern Kuangtung.

Japan: Fukien.

France: Yünnan, Kuangsi, western Kuangtung.

It should be clear by now that the expansion of the Chinese empire was not the result of a peaceful process of colonization, but the outcome of irregular thrusts, some defensive, some offensive. Colonization usually followed only after considerable delay. The country's present-day composition is the result of alternating expansion and contraction, throughout which the political and cultural heartland, the 'Eighteen Provinces' of the Ch'ing period, steadily grew. Several primary and secondary centres, that is, centres at times respectively of expansion and of contraction, can be located within the overall structure, and the pattern of fluctuation between these centres reveals a high degree of regularity. The affinity and tension between the Shensi basin (the first primary centre) and the upper North Chinese plain (the first secondary centre) have already been described. From the Chou to the T'ang, successive dynasties preferred to hold on to the region within the passes for their personal domains and later for the site of their capital (Western Chou, Ch'in, Early Han, Sui, the first half of the T'ang dynasty). The self-contained nature of the region, its economic unity and military and political cohesiveness, made it strategically superior to any other region in the period when the

47

administrative system was still in its infancy; and nearly all the major dynasties originated there (Chou, Ch'in, Han, Sui, T'ang). The plains, on the other hand, were a region of contraction and retreat. The political centre regularly moved there whenever the dynasty was threatened with isolation or overthrow within the passes, which could only be held at full strength (Eastern Chou, Later Han, the second half of the T'ang). The move to the plains often ensured survival of the dynasty for a time, but it often also entailed the loss of effective power, since its position in the geographical centre of the realm meant that the defence of the periphery had to be handed over to strong governors.

There was a fundamental shift in the position of the empire's centre at the end of the tenth century. The land within the passes lost its importance. Right from the start, the Sung established their capital in the geographical centre of north China, in fact within the limits of the first secondary centre, at Pien (now Kaifeng, Honan). Their choice was interpreted by the traditionalists as a sign of weakness. But it is also possible to regard it as ideally suitable in a period when congruence between the political centre and the military border zone was in any case out of the question, while adequate communications with the Yangtse plains, which had meanwhile become the main centre of production, must have been desirable. This deliberate choice of a new centre is less significant than the next move, forced upon the Sung by the advance of the Chin-Tartars, into the productive region of the lower Yangtse and thus to the vicinity of the coast. This ranks as the second secondary region; it had already been the refuge of the 'Chinese' dynasties in the period of the division of north from south. The Sung established their new 'temporary' capital ('stopping place' – hsing-tsai: Marco Polo's Quinsai) at Lin-an (modern Hangchou, Chekiang) in 1138. Ever since, apart from times of crisis such as the Second World War, the political centre of China has always been near the sea (Hangchou for the Southern Sung, Peking for the Yüan, Nanking and Peking for the Ming, Peking for the Ch'ing, Peking for the republic, Nanking for the Nationalists, Peking for the People's Republic). The shift can hardly be regarded, however, as a conscious turn towards the sea.

That the rulers of China became more aware of the sea as a sphere of activity and an important frontier, was a consequence of moving the political centre, not the motive for it. From the point of view of political geography the Sung period was one of transition. This is

48

revealed not least by what the contemporary historiographers had to say about the relationship between the geopolitical base and the legitimacy of a dynasty. Until that time the capital's position had been one of the criteria of a regime's legitimacy. Now it gave place once and for all to the principle of blood-relationship. The question had first been raised in the Chin period. There had been no authoritative answer, however, until provided by Chu Hsi. The verdict of the age of the Western Chin on the three preceding rival dynasties was that the Wei had been the legitimate dynasty because they had received the throne from the Han and had ruled over the nucleus of the Han empire, the Huangho plains. The Shu, however, had been based in the peripheral region of Ssechuan (the third secondary centre) and the Wu in the remote Yangtse plains (the second secondary centre). This view was shared by Ssu-ma Kuang, a minister of the Northern Sung, whose centre was also in the Huangho plains. When the Chin were forced to move southwards they set up their capital in the vicinity of the modern city of Nanking. New criteria of legitimacy became necessary and blood-relationship replaced territorialism. The Eastern Chin regarded the Shu as the legal heirs of the Han, and this view was shared by Chu Hsi, a minister of the Southern Sung, who found themselves in a similar situation to the Eastern Chin. Chu Hsi's authority helped dissipate totally the almost mystical political significance of the Huangho region.

But although the Yangtse region became a centre of economic and demographic gravity, it does not appear as the second primary centre from a modern standpoint. That role devolves on the region around Peking, although it is well away from the centre of the nuclear Eighteen Provinces. The hydrographic situation of the region was particularly good, compared with many parts of north China. It had also been the political centre of all the major foreign dynasties (Liao-Kitan, Chin-Jurchen, Yüan-Mongols), long before the third Ming emperor, Ch'eng-tsu (reigned 1403–25), moved his capital there from Nanking. The foreigners' preference for the flat, dry plains around Peking may well have been the outcome of their nomadic origins on the central Asian steppes. It is not impossible therefore that removal of the Ming political centre to the economic and demographic periphery was intended partly to serve a symbolic purpose, as though the act of occupying the enemy's base would exorcize the enemy himself. The primary reasons for the move were of course strategic; both personal, since the emperor's own power was drawn from the locality,

49

and dynastic, since Peking was in the immediate vicinity of the northern frontier, which was always at risk, and of the Nan-k'ou Pass, the most important of the routes by which the Mongols might attack. Peking was an ideal base for the foreign dynasties, including the Ch'ing-Manchu. It was inside the Great Wall, but at the same time was not too far from their homelands. Under foreign government it was particularly important for Peking to fill the double role of capital of China and capital of the peripheral, central Asian regions. Peking lay on the boundary between these two differing geographic and cultural spheres; it was intended to link them, and it did. To this paramount end, great difficulties had to be endured in keeping the cities supplied from the distant centres of production. Till the beginning of the second millennium AD the political centre had always been in one of the key economic regions, of which the alluvial land flanking the Huangho, the Yangtse lowlands and the Ssechuan basin were the most important. The choice of Peking put an end to that once and for all.

3 Demography

The population of a country, as society's fundamental material substratum, is far more significant to the historical process than the country's physical nature itself. Alterations to the population of a historical continuum as a whole, like changes in individual social groups and cells, both result from and in turn affect historical processes; the same applies even to the very earliest periods, the survivals of which are the 'pre'-historic clues, sometimes supplemented by mythology, by which we may trace the outlines of the oldest communities and groups. The developments of 'pre'-history and early history are not outside history, though their pace is relatively very slow, so that changes are hardly perceptible. Moreover the generally more modest sources of information about early historical phases need investigation with techniques different from those appropriate to the more advanced stages of civilization belonging to 'historical time in the narrower sense' (Heuss). But even with the advanced cultures it is usually impossible to quantify clearly natural movements of the population, the migration or cohesion of any one social cell or group, until the most recent period, that is, until the age of total quantification. Even tracing alterations to the constitution of the population as a whole is subject to restrictions. Early sources only refer, almost without exception, to the tip of the social pyramid and mention the rest of it, at best, indirectly.

ARCHAEOLOGICAL FINDS AND ANCIENT TRADITIONS

The discovery of 'Peking Man' at Chou-k'ou-tien near Peking in 1929 demonstrated that the region was already inhabited by hominids 400,000 years ago; and yet older finds were unearthed in recent years estimated to date back some 600,000 years. There is still no complete

51

agreement on what 'Peking Man' looked like. It has been suggested that the anatomical characteristics of *Sinanthropis pekinensis* display mongoloid features (Black, Weidenreich). The cave at Chou-k'ou-tien contained the remains of over forty people, a remarkable number. From the palaeanthropological data, Henri Breuil made a pictorial reconstruction, depicting Peking Men living as a quasi-organized group (1945).

The next oldest anthropological finds date from a substantially later period (20,000 to 25,000 years BC). The sites are in the area of Shensi and Mongolia to the south of the Ordos loop of the Huangho, and in a stratum of earth above the cave of Chou-k'ou-tien. It has not yet proved possible to establish a direct link between these finds and the beginnings of Chinese culture. It is not even absolutely certain when the 'Neolithic Revolution' (Childe) – the process during which man became settled in a particular area, creating the subsequent culture of the region – took place in China.

The oldest artefacts date from the third millennium BC. The ceramics are regarded as particularly characteristic. They are attributed to two separate cultures of late Neolithic farming communities: the Yang-shao culture (Honan, Shansi, Shensi, Kansu), whose red ware displays a certain similarity to early ceramic finds from northern and central Asia and from south-east Europe, and the Lung-shan culture (Honan, Shantung, Kiangsu, Anhui), whose pottery is typically monochrome black. In addition to the ceramic survivals finds have included an abundance of other artefacts (stone knives, spearheads), the traces of settlements (cave dwellings, earth walls of later dates) and remains of food (bones of pigs and dogs, and of sheep and cattle from later periods). Some are comparable to finds in western Asia and the Mediterranean area beyond and in south-east Asia too. Others are radically different from any of these. Adoptions from foreign cultures and autochthonous developments may have taken place simultaneously and in neighbouring areas.

The two cultures appear to have overlapped, and may have intermingled, in the An-yang area (Honan). Large amounts of a grey ceramic ware have been found there, and this is believed to belong to the transitional Hsiao-t'un culture (first half of the second millennium BC). An-yang lies in the centre of the alluvial region which later formed the heartland of China, the Central Plains. Wolfram Eberhard postulates that in early historical times there were eight individual local cultures settled around the geographical centre, the region of the

52

middle course of the Huangho. It was, he asserts, in this same central area that intercultural influences and borrowings allowed the development of the superior culture which was eventually understood as Chinese. These factors were less important, in Karl Wittfogel's view. He considers that Chinese civilization developed from the interplay of forces necessary to the agricultural cultivation of the region, above all from the organization of labour essential to irrigation and drainage projects. It is questionable, however, whether the 'hydraulic society' theory is applicable at so early a date. Arable farming remained essentially dependent on rainfall until well into the Chou period, and artificial irrigation on a large scale was not introduced until the first millennium BC.

Five hundred years before that development started, the region about An-yang already enjoyed a mature Bronze Age culture. The first step in its discovery was when peasants started ploughing up curiously inscribed bones towards the end of the nineteenth century. To begin with, most of them found their way to apothecaries and drug-makers, as prophylactic 'dragons' bones'. But by the turn of the century Chinese scholars were taking an interest in the inscriptions (Wang Kuo-wei, Lo Chen-yü). They discovered that the characters were early forms of those that are still in use. Systematic excavation between 1929 and 1933 brought whole 'archives' of inscribed bones to light, as well as dozens of inscribed bronze vessels, numerous burial sites with the bones of humans and animals, and the remains of war chariots, weapons and foodstuffs. Evaluation of these finds – still not fully completed – resulted in a multidimensional picture of early Chinese society. Some of the details may be disputable, but that it was undoubtedly a 'Chinese' society was one of the most important discoveries. The inscriptions on the bronze vessels and on the bones (mostly the shoulder blades of mammals and tortoise shells, used to record oracles) enabled the compilation of a chronology of rulers, corresponding in general to the genealogy of the Shang dynasty. This was probably transmitted orally and written down for the first time by Ssu-ma Ch'ien a thousand years later. Thus, at almost exactly the same moment when the historical reliability of traditional accounts of the period before 1000 BC was being seriously questioned, it was confirmed, at least for the Shang period. It is supposed that this particular kind of oracle already existed before the Shang dynasty. Other striking developments of earlier stylistic elements, such as the tripod Li vessel, were rediscovered in the Shang finds. The continuing influence of very early elements in the early historical phase makes the Shang appear as at least the spiritual heirs of the black and grey ceramic cultures. At the same time obviously new elements and techniques, such as the cultivation of wheat and the construction of war chariots, were adopted at first or second hand from other regions. Other developments were original, such as the *t'ao-t'ieh* masks – symmetrical, frontal representations of the features of animals, as if skinned and flattened on either side of the nose. This kind of mask is unknown in the early historical West, and known only at later dates in the Pacific area and among the Indians of north-west America. Many of the detailed aspects of Shang society remain obscure. It was probably protofeudal, with the beginnings of a hierarchic system of administration. If so, the Shang stood on the threshold of an advanced culture, in which concentration of power in one hand, with administrative departmentalization and planning, had already been completed. It is likely that the area ruled by the Shang chief was no more than two or three hundred square miles, in which the mass of the population were arable farmers living in isolated villages in Neolithic conditions. It seems to have been a 'city state', in which succession was fratrilinear. The excavations yielded evidence of human sacrifice and the worship of both ancestors and nature gods. One of the gods was the 'supreme deified ancestor' (*Shang-ti*; later a title of the Chinese emperor). It seems reasonably certain that cowrie shells, probably from the region south of the Yangtse, were used as a medium of exchange. Stylistic elements derived from forest animals and game figure prominently. This was interpreted for a while as an indication that the Shang might have come from the forest to the south of the Huangho plains. But all these individual traits are of small significance historically, compared to the large number of social, economic and cultural elements which survived from the Shang period to the end of the empire, whether the script, the dominance of agriculture or the functional organization of the community.

A second centre of early Chinese culture was discovered among the mountain passes of the Shensi basin. Chinese archaeologists have suggested that the people who occupied this region at the time of the Shang are to be identified with the people of the red ceramic culture, but this has not earned complete acceptance. Inscribed oracle bones have been found in this area too, but that would suggest a relationship with the Shang, if anything. It is possible that they are in fact Shang survivals, left behind after an attempt at conquest. The proof of the relative independence of this cultural nucleus seems rather to lie in the fact that a society grew up here which, for all its resemblance to the Shang culture, possessed characteristics generally derived from the greater proximity of the 'barbarian' pastoral races to the west and north. That culture in turn is occasionally regarded as being of central Asian origin, although there is little evidence to support the view.

The picture of this society, which is now called Chou, becomes clearer towards the end of the first millennium BC. The Chou King Wen (traditionally 1231–1135 BC) was simultaneously the Shang Lord of the Western Marches (Hsi-po). In 1122 BC (the traditional date; in the second half of the tenth century BC, according to modern research) King Wu, the son of King Wen, rose against the Shang, toppled their ruler and conquered the Central Plains. This event came to have a far greater significance than the overthrow of one power by another, in that it was the example that legitimized every subsequent change of dynasty for nearly three thousand years. The Chou justified their breach of faith by the claim that the Shang had forfeited their sovereignty by their worsening depravity, culminating in the monstrous person of the 'last ruler', and that the 'mandate of heaven' (*t'ien-ming*) had thereupon fallen to them. 'Heaven' (*t'ien*) was the chief Chou deity, though 'heaven' is a very imprecise equivalent to the Chinese concept of *t'ien* at this early date. It is likely that *t'ien* was of anthropomorphic origin, like *shang-ti*, and probably meant 'ancestor', or more specifically, 'ancestor of the Chou'. The Chou rulers, and all the later kings and emperors of China, called themselves the 'sons of heaven' (*t'ien-tzu*); the order of succession among the Chou was patrilinear. It appears, too, that the Chou found little difficulty in identifying their *t'ien* with the Shang god *shang-ti*, which also seems to corroborate an origin of that kind.

The Chou were not yet in a position to exercise direct rule over the newly conquered territory. Their authority reached essentially no further than their own kingdom within the mountain passes. They put the Central Plains under the rule of vassals, most of them their own kinsmen, though a few were loyal local princes and other followers not linked by ties of blood. It is not quite clear whether this was a genuine feudal system; it may have been no more than a rearrangement of the earlier tribal organization around a ceremonial centre. The 'fiefs' of the vassals, which are believed to have numbered more than a hundred to begin with, probably each consisted at first of a walled fortress-town and the land around it.

As little is known for certain about early Chou society as about the Shang. There was clearly a deep gulf between the prince and the common people. Apart from his kinsmen, the people closest to the prince were the 'Great Dignitaries' (*tai-fu*), a circle of people from whom the warriors and priest-scribes were probably also recruited. The mass of the population, the literally nameless peasant farmers, were the serfs of the vassal governors, and had to pay tribute in kind and carry out statute labour. They probably still lived in late Stone Age conditions, as under the Shang, supporting themselves in their villages. As far as can be seen, slavery played hardly any part in production.

Until archaeological evidence came to light, the early period was known only through mythological and historical traditions. These were rejected as fictive, until the discovery and decipherment of the oracle bones confirmed the traditional account of the Shang dynasty, which had been first written down a thousand years later. The same written source, the *Shih-chi* of Ssu-ma Ch'ien, also mentions an even earlier dynasty, the Hsia (traditional dating 2205–1766 BC; also 1994–1523 BC). Archaeology has so far failed to furnish evidence of the historicity of this dynasty. However, the rediscovery of the Shang means that its existence cannot be ruled out altogether.

The traditional Chinese chronology goes even further back, but it becomes noticeably more detailed towards the end of the first millennium BC than at its beginning. The oldest written sources, the *Book of Songs* (*Shih-ching*) and the *Book of Documents* (*Shu-ching*), which date wholly or partly from the first half of the first millennium BC, contain very little about the period before 1000 BC. Only with the increase of written sources does information about the early period become more detailed. One reason for this may be that as human existence became more reasoning and aware, parties with political interests adapted elements of the tradition so as to increase their own influence, or to give their own ideas a historical, though not transcendental, pedigree. Where the tradition has been reworked in this way, details sometimes differ to a considerable degree. Generally, though, they conform to the same pattern. In the beginning there was P'an-ku, the creator of heaven and earth. He was succeeded by twelve celestial rulers, eleven terrestrial rulers and nine human rulers. This line of succession suggests references to systems of cosmology and numerical mysticism which are typical of Chinese thought, especially at a later date. The three groups were referred to together as the 'Three Sublime Ones' (*San-huang*). In some sources the Three Sublime Ones are three individuals who succeeded to the celestial, terrestrial and human rulers. They were followed by the 'Five Divine [Emperors]' (*Wu-ti*), who included probably the most famous of all the rulers in the Chinese tradition, the 'Yellow Emperor' (*Huang-ti*) and two model potentates, Yao and Shun. The cultural developments of the greatest importance to later Chinese were attributed to these rulers. They were represented, that is, as benefactors of society and the community. The skills they created and passed on include making fire, building houses, tilling the ground, preparing medicines, drawing up the calendar and making written records of events and thoughts. The order in which these cultural advances are listed is a perfectly feasible sequence of development, of 'civilization', according to the present state of our knowledge. One of the deeds attributed to Yao may well be an example of political criticism by a later emendator, directed against the patrilinear succession of the Chou dynasty: he is said to have passed over his weak and incapable son in favour of the virtuous and able Shun, a fisherman and a peasant. Similarly, Shun is said to have appointed his minister Yü as his successor. Yü is the last of the line of rulers to whom benefits of mythological magnitude are attributed, in his case the drainage and irrigation of the flood plains in which his people lived. With Yü the tradition enters on a new phase, it becomes more concrete. The members of the Hsia dynasty, which he is alleged to have founded, ruled for feasible numbers of years, unlike their predecessors, whose spans were of Old Testament proportions. According to the tradition the Hsia dynasty eventually became degenerate and was overthrown by the people around the middle of the second millennium BC. It was followed by the Shang dynasty, whose existence is supported by archaeological evidence, as has been shown. The historicity of a Hsia dynasty is not rejected out of hand. Generally, however, it is assumed that the tradition relating to it was fabricated by the Chou in order to legitimize their own rebellion against the Shang. There is a little evidence which suggests that the Hsia may have been contemporaries and neighbours of the Shang.

It was above all the Chinese scholars of the sceptical school of the early twentieth century, who questioned the early traditions. They discovered, in the details in particular, intentional back projections from the Time of the Warring States. In spite of these caveats, however, the traditional accounts, embellished with all the details, are still sometimes related as part of the 'Five-thousand-year-old history of China' (Chang Ch'i-yün).

POPULATION AND SOCIETY

The population during the Chou period of the territories later regarded as Chinese is not known. Some of the sources give figures, such as 13·7 million at the beginning of the dynasty, and 11·8 million for the year 684 BC. However, these are not accepted by scholars, because they cannot be verified. The earliest population count accepted as verifiable is the levy of the year 2 BC. The population of the Han empire at that date was alleged to be 59·5 million (57·6 million after arithmetical correction). The majority of these people lived in the Shensi basin, on the south side of the Huangho in the upper lowlands, and along the Min River in Ssechuan. Hans Bielenstein believes that this number was the product of a genuine census based on the 'Household Registers' (*hu-tse*), and not simply the total of persons listed in the taxation registers as liable for tax. He thus contradicts the view that population levies in traditional China only served basically fiscal purposes, and that the figures they give are therefore always lower than the actual total. This differing interpretation certainly offers a plausible explanation of the immense fluctuations shown by the figures. There is another explanation, however, namely when the figures are taken from 'tax lists' (*chi-chang*) pure and simple. The 'taxable population' (later *ting, ting-k'ou*) generally consisted only of men within certain age limits. Tax-exempt persons, such as women, children, old men, invalids, soldiers, slaves, civil servants, noblemen and at certain times monks, were therefore omitted from the lists. If taxable individuals entered the service of the tax-exempt they had to be struck off the list. It is not always easy to tell in isolated cases whether a change in the total is attributable to a fluctuation in the taxable population or to different methods of computation. In no case, however, should a great discrepancy between two figures be interpreted simply as a drop or rise in the total population, as happens in many works. Such a discrepancy is found among the figures for the Later Han period. The total for AD 57 is given as 21 million and that for AD 105 as 53·2 million. The distribution of the population had altered fundamentally since the Former Han period. The north-west, the Shensi basin, had lost nearly 6·5 million inhabitants; the north-east, the lowlands, had lost as many as 11 million. The south, on the other hand, especially the large valleys of what were later Kiangsi and Hunan, had acquired approximately 11 million. Two principal reasons can be given: invasions in the north-west by alien races and the removal of the capital city, and a major change in the course of the Huangho in the lowlands.

Population movement in the period between the Han and the T'ang is obscure. A levy of c. AD 300 gives a sum total of 16·1 million; like most of the counts of this period it was probably a taxation levy. There is almost a complete dearth of statistics about population shifts at this time, too. It is known, however, that large numbers migrated to the south from the north-west, driven by foreign invasions, and settled principally in the valleys south of the Yangtse, in the coastal regions (Fukien), and in some other peripheral areas (Kansu, Ssechuan). As in the Later Han period, loss of population in one region was balanced by an almost equivalent increase in another. The total population remained relatively stable. Migrations were instigated and directed by the government only very rarely. On the contrary: the rulers regarded movements by the mass of the population as a danger, to be prevented. Migration from the north meant temporary or permanent additions to the population of the south. Losses in the north by and large impaired political stability. On the other hand the spread of Chinese elements in the south resulted in an ethnographical balance which contributed to the unity of the whole area in the long run.

The total population is estimated to have been 48 million under the Sui dynasty. North China still dominated with about 75 per cent; the south, from the middle Yangtse to the Pearl River, held only about 10 per cent.

The registers listed 52·8 million people in the year 754. A list dated only ten years later gives only 16·9 million. This drop has been linked with the conflict ensuing from the rebellion of An Lu-shan (755) (by Giles; more recently by Franke/Trauzettel). However, it is very doubtful whether this short period of unrest, violent though it undeniably was, could have resulted in so many deaths. It is more likely that the second list was only a tax register, regarded as more urgent after the disturbances than a proper census. After the unification of the empire by the Sui and T'ang the population of the north-west again became denser. The capital was moved back to the Shensi basin. More than a million people lived within its walls. The total including the inhabitants of the suburbs was 2 million. The Huangho plain gradually filled up too. At the same time, Ssechuan and the Yangtse region remained densely populated. After the period, following the fall of the Han, when the north and south were divided, the T'ang period was the third phase in which settlement of the south progressed. In the middle of the eighth century only about 50 per cent of the population still lived in the north. The total area was thus more evenly populated under the T'ang rulers than at any previous time.

The total population in the early twelfth century is estimated at about 100 million. It is impossible to calculate with absolute certainty whether the population increased more rapidly under the Sung than in earlier centuries. Probably, however, the continuing opening up of the south (which had, at the end of the thirteenth century, 85 per cent of the population), technical and agrarian advances (the adoption of fast-growing varieties of rice from south-east Asia) and growth in inland and overseas trade, could all have stimulated population growth. Another characteristic of the Sung period was a completely new trend towards urbanization. There had been large agglomerated settlements before then, but in virtually every case they had been the successive capital cities. But now cities of a million or more inhabitants sprang up in quite a short period in the provinces too. Suchou (Kiangsu), for instance, had a population of over 2·5 million by around the year 1200. This development reflected a general shift in the social centre of gravity from the country to the town. No longer was a town merely the district centre for marketing and administration. It became the focal point for all aspects of the way of life and the place where the landowning classes preferred to take up residence.

One of the most thorough population counts was carried out under the first Ming emperor, T'ai-tsu (reigned 1368–98). It produced the total of 60·5 million for the year 1393. Ho Ping-ti has shown, however, that even this census varied markedly in efficiency from region to region, and that the figure is probably below the real total. The numbers actually fell during the Ming regime, although the empire was relatively peaceful, there were no insurrections of any significance and the registered area of land under cultivation grew by 30 per cent. It is therefore assumed that a considerable part of the population disappeared into the anonymity of employment by the privileged landowners, while the real total grew steadily from over 65 million, or perhaps as much as 100 million, to approximately 150 million. This is the figure given in the official sources as late as the first half of the eighteenth century, while it is very nearly up to 450 million by the middle of the nineteenth. This represents a threefold increase in the size of the population in a little over a hundred years: a most unusual rate of growth for a pre-industrial society. For this reason the figure of 150 million is usually assumed for a rather earlier period, some time in the seventeenth century. The fact remains that there was a substantial population increase in the first half of the Ch'ing period. On the one hand this is attributed to internal peace and stability. On the other it is considered due to the opening up of virgin territory, the introduction of new crops such as maize, tobacco, sweet potatoes, ground nuts and yet more new varieties of rice and possibly to improvements in hygiene as well. At all events the limits of self-sufficiency were reached with a population of 250 million between about 1750 and 1775. The outcome was overpopulation. In the second half of the eighteenth century, probably not for the first time, China went beyond the critical point at which there was an ideal balance of the number of its inhabitants and the productivity possible at that time. While the population continued to grow rapidly, productivity lagged behind. The increase in population was greeted at first as a gift from heaven. But already by the turn of the century, ways were sought to slow it down, since a corresponding increase in the means of production which, to the traditional Chinese official mind, primarily meant new land and new methods of cultivation, appeared unattainable. The consequences were a sharp fall in the standard of living, extremely rapid growth of unemployment and a swift increase in the number of groups living on the fringes of society. As early as 1820 the traditional social categories of civil servants, farmers, craftsmen and merchants are supposed to have accounted for little more than half the total population. The element of instability thus introduced into Chinese society presented potentially a major threat to the continuance of the existing order. The government, or at least some officials in positions of authority, were fully aware of the problems involved and tried to alleviate local population pressures by promoting resettlement. Substantial numbers of peasants moved from the overpopulated province of Kuangtung into Kuangsi as early as the turn of the century. After the Taiping rebellion the Manchu homeland, Manchuria, was opened up to Chinese settlers, primarily from Shantung and the north Chinese lowlands. This particular move also served strategic purposes, since Russia had begun to establish outposts in the region to the north and east of Amur and Ussuri. But these

61

measures, like the permission given to imperial subjects to emigrate to the new colonies in south-east Asia and later to the United States, or to prospect in the mountains – which was regarded as an 'unorthodox' occupation – produced relief only at the regional level. Some people took such a despairing view of the situation that they recommended a relaxation of the laws against infanticide, a ban on widows remarrying, female sterilization by means of drugs, the raising of the minimum age for marriage, special taxation of families with more than two children and the drowning of all 'superfluous' children. Clearly the growth of the population was catastrophic not only for the masses, the people most directly affected, but also for the ruling classes. It could even be argued that it was the uncontrollable rise in the population, unmatched by a corresponding growth in the productive capacity and the increase in those exempt from taxation, which repeatedly most threatened the government of the day. In traditional China population growth was expected to be regulated by natural and political disasters. Foods, droughts, rebellions and wars did in fact reduce the population by a few million from time to time, allowing a certain regional relief. But over the empire as a whole, not even the enormous loss of 20 million, or perhaps even 40 million lives during the nineteenth century in a series of natural catastrophes (the change of the course of the Huangho between 1853 and 1855) and rebellions (Taiping, Nien, Moslems), did anything to alleviate population pressures to any significant degree. The problem was inherited by the new China of the twentieth century.

The smallest group in any society is the family. In traditional China too, it was the family which was the basic socio-political unit, not the individual. A family consisted theoretically of five generations and five degrees of kinship. Great-great-grandparents, great-great-grandchildren and third cousins were all included. Ideally this enlarged family group, organized on strictly patriarchal lines, lived together under one roof. But this can seldom actually have been the case, even with well-to-do families, quite apart from the age differences between the oldest and the youngest generations. It was more common for all the members of one family to live in the same place. The family, as the basic social cell, founded on kinship, was then identical with the next basic unit, the community founded on neighbourhood. (Let it be said at this juncture that a local or regional association (*t'ung-hsiang*), even when not based on kinship, still induced a sense of very close community among the Chinese.) The traditional Chinese family was not only a domestic unit. It was also an economic and religious unit, and acknowledged corporate liability. There was hardly any personal property. All income went to the family. In return the family guaranteed each member sustenance. If a member of a family earned fame and honours, it was his duty to share his good fortune with the others. This was one of the causes of the much-deplored nepotism in the traditional Chinese civil service. The position of the family determined social status; a move within the social structure, that is, social mobility, affected the whole family. To leave one's family was tantamount to leaving society. Even after death a member of a family remained bound to it as a 'spirit'; the veneration of ancestors in general was the ultimate sign of family unity. The family was legally responsible for all its members' actions. It was thus the nucleus of political control of the state, since, fixed in one place, it was more vulnerable to retribution at the hands of authority than a mobile individual. In historical times the Chinese family was never merely a 'natural' cell, but always a politically shaped, politically relevant sub-group. It is not possible to deduce exactly when the family as described here became the norm, the type to which the population as a whole, over and beyond the uppermost level of society, conformed. It was already the subject of eager discussion by the end of the Chou period, demonstrated by the backward projection of appropriate family virtues to the 'founders' of the Chinese family, the legendary rulers Fu-hsi and Yao.

One of the most controversial questions in the field of Chinese history is whether and when there was a slave-owning society. Marxist historians have no doubt as to the answer to the primary question; their sole concern is to fix its dates. The hypothesis that there was a slave-owning society in the Shang period is supported above all by the numerous burial sites that have been found containing the remains of 'companions' to the chief occupant of the grave, who were either buried alive or decapitated first (Kuo Mo-jo). According to the tradition these unfortunates were generally prisoners-of-war, which does not rule out the possibility of their having been used as slaves first. Whether society under the Chou should be described as slave-owning is more hotly debated (Fan Wön-lan). Undoubtedly there were slaves in the early period, but it is open to question whether they represented the great majority of the labour force. This question is dependent, however, on the definition of slavery. Production was at all events mainly the work of serfs. It is also beyond doubt that in both the Shang and the Chou periods a huge social and economic gulf separated the high from the low. The social cleft was later formularized by the apologists for the traditional order, the Confucians, in such expressions as 'ceremonial rites do not touch the common people; legal penalties do not touch high dignitaries'. It was still maintained even when the main producers, first in Ch'in (from 400 BC) and later in the whole empire (from 200 BC), became in large number the owners of the soil they cultivated. This development was not initiated and repeatedly repromoted in order to benefit the farmers, but in order to increase the state's revenues. Even after the 'liberation of the peasants', the great mass of the people who lived by tilling the soil only concerned the state, whoever held power, in the capacity of taxpayers, statute labourers and potential rebels. In spite of their importance as the principal means of production they remained an underprivileged class of Chinese society until very recently. They had their own customs, their own religious cults, their own pantheon of demons. While they were guided in general by the 'great tradition' laid down by the upper classes, they lived in a social 'popular' world of the 'little tradition' (Redfield), which differed from the 'great' tradition more in externals than in fundamentals. It was however, the 'great' tradition which for many centuries purported to be the true Chinese way, especially when it came to impressing the outside world. Social mobility within the farmers' class meant primarily movement between the alternatives of being an underprivileged landowner or a tenant farmer, very often under a double obligation to the state and to the landlord. If a peasant became a serf he was excluded from the farmers' class. At every period of Chinese history the farmers represented the largest section of the population (about 90 per cent).

The proper dating of a feudal period in Chinese history is also still not agreed. Marxist historians hold that feudalism in China began with the end of the slave-owning society of the early era. This dates it from the Chou dynasty; and some of them maintain that it lasted into the nineteenth century. They define feudalism less by the principles of formal vassalage as by the relationship between those who owned the land and those who worked it – by production through exploitation of serfs or tenants by the landowner. On the whole, non-Marxist historians reject this view. But they have not generally agreed on an alternative dating. The indications of vassalage that have survived from both the Shang and the Chou periods have already been mentioned. There is, however, very little evidence as to the detailed working of these relationships. What is known is based essentially on accounts written down at a much later date, notably by the Confucian school of historians, who may well have idealized the situation. On the basis of this group of sources, some historians warn against assuming that there was a fully developed feudal system, based on legal and contractual principles, under the Chou (Reischauer/Fairbank). They believe the system at that date was no more than an extension of the traditional organization along tribal and family lines, deriving its authority less from legal principles than from blood-relationships. Another school of thought sees power as the central factor: the Chinese feudal society was founded and shaped by the superimposition of a new order (the Chou) on an existing society (the Shang) (Eberhard). This society was characterized by a clear distinction between the rulers and the ruled, the ruling class at least being hierarchically organized. It is unimportant whether the rulers were of the same tribe or not. If this view is valid, then the Chou period must be designated a feudal one. The ruling class, the Chou 'nobility', was distinguished from the overthrown Shang and from their subjects not only by its political power but also racially, with a few exceptions. This apparently promoted a series of factors which provided the basis and the definition of the exclusiveness of the ruling class, over and above their position of power. The nobility had its own religion, the worship of heaven. This could only be celebrated by the 'Son of Heaven', the highest secular lord. The people, the ruled, had no part in it. This practice, too, was later raised by the Confucian apologists to a central principle of the state religion of imperial China. Endogamy, which was the rule at that date, may also have originated in the same way, in the Chou tradition of ethnic exclusivity. There were special legal norms, moral principles and rites (*li*) for the nobility, that consisted of precedents and analogies. The common people were subject to a penal code with fixed conditions and penalties. Only the nobility were entitled to passage of arms.

In consequence of social differentiation, an intermediate class emerged in the middle of the Chou period between the rulers and the ruled, sooner in some states than in others. Its members acted on behalf of the rulers as executives, or functionaries, and gained an increasing amount of power and influence. The new class was composed partly of the prince's high officers of state and their assistants, and partly of free merchants and of warriors of noble blood, who, although they were not vassals, had made themselves useful to the prince as tax-collectors. Later, when the emperors succeeded in

65

depriving the feudal nobility of their power, these too sank to the level of the new class. Although they gradually lost their political rights, the nobility remained for the most part the landlords (*ti-chu*) of considerable estate and constituted the favoured source of candidates for high office. The process went on until the T'ang period. The central ruler was not infrequently compelled to restore some of their ancient privileges to the nobility: for instance, at the beginning of the Han regime. After the T'ang period titles of nobility were in practice reserved for members of the ruling house. Deserving officers of state were rewarded by elevation to a nominal nobility, which did not form a social class of any significance.

The centralization of power from the Ch'in period onwards brought with it social changes which affected other classes besides the nobles. After the transfer of land was permitted, many families of humble origins succeeded in amassing great wealth by accumulating land. These new rich created another source of recruitment for the civil service. Noble blood ceased to be a *sine qua non* for holding office, although the qualifications required from the first century BC onwards served only as a limited criterion until the Sung period. The privileges of powerful and influential families, though these were now by no means all of noble descent, continued to dominate for the time being. Whether these families are properly called 'gentry' as early as the Han period (Eberhard/Teng Ssu-yü) is open to doubt. They were certainly the origin of the social class that came to dominate the life of traditional China, reaching its peak in the second millennium AD. This upper stratum between rulers and ruled must be defined as much by its possessions as by its administrative functions. It was the possessions rather than the functions that established membership of the class under the Han rulers and throughout almost the whole of the period up to about the year 1000. Thereafter it was rather the other way round, but the elitism of wealth remained characteristic of the class. An office could only be taken by passing the prescribed state examinations. Qualifying in the examinations was only open to someone who had access to a certain minimum of wealth, that is, someone whose family could afford to do without the labour of one of its members and still produce an economic surplus. Leisure was essential to self-improvement and education. In other words, the rich and the very rich had a monopoly of education. Vertical social mobility was theoretically possible, but extremely rare in practice.

The upper class defined by wealth and function assumed some of the distinguishing marks and privileges of the old nobility. The state official and landowner was separated from the common farmer, craftsman and merchant by as broad a gulf as previously existed between the nobleman and the commoner. The substantial material benefits attendant on social prestige, in the form of preferential taxation and exemption from statute service, effectively create a direct link between the aristocracy of blood of the Chou era, the aristocracy of wealth of the first millennium AD and the aristocracy of education of the second. From the Sung period at least, however, membership of the upper class ceased to be by inheritance alone. The right to it had to be proved anew in each generation by qualifying in the system of state examinations, the 'ladder of success' (Ho Ping-ti). As a result an individual family might lose its status, but the ruling class as a whole retained its monopolistic hold on the administration. It survived every political upheaval until the twentieth century. It was indispensable to the head of state as the intermediary between the ruler and the ruled. In view of its capacity for survival and its crucial role in the exercise of government, it must be acknowledged as the true master of traditional China; it was the upholder of the 'great tradition' of Chinese society. Yet it rarely accounted for more than 2 per cent of the entire population. In view of its function under the later dynasties it is not inappropriate to call it a civil service.

The civil service and the farmers were the most important social classes of traditional China. They occupied respectively first and second place among the Four Estates (*ssu-min*) into which Chinese society was traditionally divided. The system of division, and the priorities governing it, reached far back into the Chou era, though it was not always in the same order: civil service (warriors in early times), farmers, craftsmen, merchants (*shih, nung, kung, shang*). According to some of the sources there was a time, and probably only in certain regions, when the merchants came second, after the warriors. This evaluation was probably linked with the temporary employment of some merchants as assistants to the administration, as tax-collectors. It was exceptional; for more than two thousand years the merchant was regarded as the most dubious member of society, his occupation as the least productive and the most degraded. An 'honourable family' (*liang-chia*) did not engage in trade or similar disreputable enterprises. Quite apart from the moral justification this estimate received on the part of officials and scholars schooled in Confucianism, which above all else condemned striving for profit (*li*), the low opinion of trade

67

probably had a sound political foundation. As early as the time of the Chou wealthy merchants clearly represented a considerable potential threat to the aristocratic order. They were comparatively mobile, and their wealth put them in a position to acquire power themselves. It is conceivable that this consideration played some part in assigning merchants to the lowliest position in the social order. Even after the unification of the empire, and the rise of the landowning administrative class to true power, rich merchants remained a threat, both to the administration as such and to its personal possessions. Pan Ku (32–92), author of the second of the great dynastic histories, significantly connects the fall of the Chou with the spread of trade and commerce. The distrust the Confucian upper class had of the merchants consolidated their low social standing. The whole field of commerce lacked any kind of protection by legislation. The precariousness of his legal position and his social disrepute in combination meant that the best a merchant could hope for was to invest his profits in land, and even this was not always permitted. The prohibition of land purchase was usually combined with exclusion from the state examinations and therefore from any kind of state office. Thus a deliberate attempt was made by one social class to defend its interests against another. Once again, the situation changed under the Sung emperors: in the developing urbanized society, with its dependence on trade, it was no longer possible to exclude merchants artificially from social advancement. Thereafter almost all the more prosperous merchant families tried to get some of their members into the civil service, and then to help them gain promotion, both to enhance the family's status, and to protect its commercial enterprises. The associations between the civil service and the merchant class were soon much closer and more numerous than those between the civil service and the farmers. Their continual efforts to obtain the entrée into the civil service was probably not the least of the reasons why the merchants as a class contributed little to the history of China. In spite of the numerous 'bourgeons of capitalism' to be found from the Sung period onwards, they did not evolve into the capitalist middle class, independent of the government, that shaped the history of Europe.

The craftsmen never counted for much in the social fabric; it is even debatable whether they can be described as an independent social class at all. They were certainly regarded as such in China. Their distinguishing function was even given a precise definition: craftsmen were those who processed the raw materials produced by

68

the farmers. But so far as the organization of their work was concerned, and in the eyes of the law, a majority of the people assigned to this class were in fact those who were compelled to work for the administration, either permanently or for fixed terms, in the state manufactories of porcelain and silk, for instance; they were thus servants of the state. There were of course some independent craftsmen as well. From the Sung period onwards a considerable number of craftsmen floated on a free labour market in some of the larger cities, like modern employees. The numbers and the proportions of the two categories are not known.

As well as the four classes already described there was always a group of professions which were not considered by orthodox opinion to belong to 'society', to the 'rightful people' (*liang-min*), at all: serfs, singing girls, actors, musicians, barbers, executioners and so on. They were the outsiders of traditional Chinese society, the 'low people' (*chien-min*).

4 Polarities and Tensions

A political continuum comprises an infinite number of historical events. Every event can be traced back to a theoretically infinite number of factors, each again the result of a multidimensional web of causes and effects. Hence the necessity, when describing any one historical continuum, of confining oneself to a small number of causal forces, macrohistorically significant, but not exclusively responsible for the historical dynamic. The forces selected will be those with a bearing on heuristic categories of interpretation, not monocausal historical determinants.

Three factors, in particular, help interpret the political development of China: tension between the centre and the periphery, tension between the ruling class and those they ruled and tension between China and the outside world. These were not the only forces determining the dynamic of Chinese history, nor were they separate from each other. But together they are one of the most important complexes of factors in Chinese history. In combination they are unique to China. That is not to say that they are untypical of the histories of other countries, but the composition of the formula varies from country to country. For instance, the tension between Japan and the outside world was comparatively insignificant, or at any rate differently accented. On the other hand China has lacked some of the polarities, such as that between Church and state, which have played so important a role in European history.

'Centre and periphery' defines a physical arena as well as a power relationship. The centre and periphery of power make up a chiefly horizontal system of relationships. Within this, the complex of the ruling powers stands out vertically from the complex of the ruled. Rulers and ruled together constitute the organism that is China, the

70

individual totality that collides both vertically and horizontally with the outside world.

CENTRE AND PERIPHERY

After their victory over the Shang, the Chou gave most of their new acquisitions to kinsmen and deserving supporters as fiefs. It is not known exactly whether, or for how long, the Chou were able to exercise any real control over their vassals. But it is quite clear that, after abandoning their original homeland in the Shensi basin and moving the royal seat in 771 BC to the vicinity of the modern town of Loyang (Honan), their rule of the area that constituted their realm was purely nominal. The real power had passed to the separate states that had formed from the fiefs, of which there were more than a hundred. Possibly a similar polycentric constellation even existed previously, under the Shang and the Western Chou regimes. The destruction of earlier units of government and their replacement resulting from the Chou conquest may have amounted merely to temporary establishment of a very loosely organized, purely formal relationship. Chinese historians, especially, are inclined to assume that there was a 'system of central rule' (*i-t'ung*), even under the Chou, and that it was a 'unified feudal rule' (Ch'ien Mu). The individual units probably consisted of no more than a nuclear settlement, a walled town (*kuo*) and the cultivated land immediately surrounding it. It is not known whether the lords of the towns were the sole owners of the land in the units, or whether it was under communal ownership, which is what appears to be meant by the 'Nine Field' (*ching-t'ien*) System mentioned by later authors. Also known as the Well-Field System, each unit is understood to have comprised eight 'families' and the local lord. This arrangement would certainly have been consistent with the particularist structure of the Chou regime. Perhaps later tradition merely meant by this system a model of the ideal direct relationship between lord and subject that was believed to have existed in the early period. The historical reality is not likely to have been so very different. As the example of the Chou themselves shows, as soon as the realm outgrew his direct economic control, the king, like the Tennō in feudal Japan, was left with nothing more than nominal influence and formal, ceremonial privileges, which withered away altogether in time. Few princes bothered to have their accession confirmed by the king in the latter part of the Chou period. If, to begin with, the

71

king symbolized the unity of 'what is under heaven' (*t'ien-hsia*) – a term that seems at first to have literally signified the elevation of the 'Son of Heaven' (*t'ien-tzu*), that is, the king, above his noble vassals – towards the end of the Chou period he hardly represented the totality of the 'civilized' world. He had long ceased to be the source of any of the impulses that really governed the world.

With the decline of the secular and the sacred authority of the Chou kings, the possibility also faded of centralizing under them the government of the states. The impulses and experiences conducive to organizing power in that way and forming large governmental structures came increasingly from the states on the periphery of the polycentric Chou civilization. Several reasons exist for these states' increased power and new style of government. They could expand, at the expense of the 'barbarians' beyond their borders; they were forced into an almost permanent conflict with these barbarians; they made an earlier and more thorough break with the introverted tradition of the central states clustered round the Chou. In short, whether from necessity or inclination, they were more receptive to political, economic and technological change than the other states.

The earliest information about a development of this kind comes from the *Spring and Autumn* period. In the seventh and sixth centuries BC, the state of Ch'i, on the eastern edge of the Huangho plains, succeeded in multiplying its territory by six, spreading over almost the whole of the Shantung peninsula. This expansion was apparently coupled with changes in the governmental organization hitherto prevailing. The first attempts are discernible at a central administration of the whole area. Ch'i is said to have divided parts of its territory not into fiefs but into functional units administered directly from the centre. The sub-units are said to have paid taxes according to a fixed scale and raised troops for the central army. Economic steps included the standardization of weights and measures and the establishment of monopolies in salt and iron. Possibly these accounts refer in all their details to actual circumstances. Alternatively they may be a programmatic idealization emanating from the Legalist school. It seems certain that in Ch'i the first moves were made away from customary practices towards consolidating the power of one of the princely houses. These moves may have been intended specifically to suppress particularist interests. Probably, too, they were initiated by the minister Kuan Chung (d. 645 BC). In spite of their increased power, the dukes of Ch'i continued to respect the nominal overlordship of the Chou.

The princes of Ch'u, whose domain lay on the middle Yangtse, did not. They had already assumed the title of king (*wang*) in the eighth century BC. In so doing they denied the Chou claim of legitimacy anxiously perpetuated by the smaller states in the centre of the 'Chinese' world. Possibly the smaller states' strenuous and unceasing defence of Chou legitimacy was an attempt to resist the expansion of the larger border states. At first the defence was directed chiefly against Ch'u, whose stance seemed particularly barbaric to the smaller princes. Not merely had it usurped the title of king, but it had also disregarded the traditional usages of civilized behaviour (*li*) and was unceremoniously annexing smaller states. The power of Ch'u and the simultaneous threat from the 'barbarian' north were, however, forces that could only be met with force, and in 681 BC nearly all the states on the Huangho plains formed an alliance. The smaller princes, and the Chou king himself, acknowledged Duke Huan, the powerful lord of Ch'i (reigned 685–643 BC), as the hegemon (*pa*) or leader of the alliance (*meng-chu*). The system of appointing an overlord was a skilful compromise between the Chou claim to power and the actual possession of power by the Ch'i. Temporarily, it stabilized the situation but eventually it had the opposite effect, when the position was seized by opponents of the alliance such as King Chuang of Ch'u (613–591 BC).

The two most powerful states in the sixth century BC were Ch'u and Chin: the one to the south, the other to the north (in the area that is now the province of Shansi) of the 'Chinese' inhabited world. The confrontations between the two giants were inconclusive. The balance of power and terror ensured a temporary stability, but the smaller states in between feared constantly for their existence. For this reason, the princes of Sung and Cheng (between the Huangho and the Huaiho), two of the smaller states who suffered particularly from the altercations, attempted to persuade Ch'u and Chin to a peace treaty. It is thought that by then the two great powers had decided not only that neither of them was really capable of military victory over the other, but also that the smaller states most closely affected would incline to the side of whichever of the two honestly and openly pursued a peace policy. A treaty was consequently concluded in 546. Once again a delicate balance guaranteed the *status quo* in the central states. But only a few decades later the situation on the north and south periphery threatened to disturb the equilibrium. A belligerent rival had grown up on the east flank of Ch'u, the state of Wu, lying downstream along the Yangtse. In 481 Wu was reckoned to be the strongest and therefore the most dangerous of the states on the edge of the 'Chinese' world. Yet barely ten years later, in 473, it succumbed to the most 'barbaric' state of the Chou alliance, Yüeh (in the modern province of Chekiang). While Ch'u was thus occupied in defending itself against the growing threat on its flank, Chin was riven by civil wars. In 453 it split into three parts and so ceased to wield any influence. At the end of the fifth century, three states were dominant: Ch'u, Ch'i and the newcomer Ch'in. The Ch'in had moved into the position vacated by the Chou in the Shensi basin.

In the course of the fourth and third centuries, all the rulers of the individual states assumed the title of king: there was no longer any central authority. The struggle for hegemony was openly declared. The Chou era entered on its most turbulent phase, called by later Chinese historians the 'Time of the Warring States'. The political centre of gravity shifted from one of the larger states to another at ever decreasing intervals. The concentration of power and the absorption of smaller states changed the picture from one decade to the next. Ch'u, in the south, annexed its neighbour Yüeh in 334. By 249, after swallowing the smaller intervening states, Ch'u reached as far as the borders of Ch'i, which had meanwhile extended towards Ch'u with the conquest of Sung in 286. While Ch'u and Ch'i thus vied with each other, Ch'in was able to expand its territory almost without interference. In 316 Ch'in subdued the semi-sinized states of Pa and Shu in the Ssechuan basin. At about the same time it struck the Chin successor states a blow from which they did not recover. In 256 the king of Chou yielded his domains to the prince of Ch'in; in 249 the last king of Chou was deposed without resistance worthy of mention from any quarter. Finally, the Ch'in king, Cheng (reigned 246–210 BC), overran the few remaining independent states, including Ch'u and Ch'i, in a lightning campaign. In 221 'what is under heaven' was subject to a single ruler. The Chinese empire dates from then, and did not formally end until 1912. The new 'Universal Ruler' of Ch'in – his domestic name (Chin-a) was adopted for the realm, in the West as well – abandoned the title of king in favour of 'Sublime and Divine One' (*huang-ti*), in reference to the 'Three Sublime' and 'Five Divine' legendary rulers of the past. The new title is normally translated as 'emperor'. As Cheng was envisaged as the first of an unending line of central rulers of Ch'in, his full title was 'First Sublime and Divine [Lord] of Ch'in' (Ch'in Shih-huang-ti).

How had this been possible? The peculiarly favourable conditions for the peripheral states' increase in power have already been pointed out. Like the other large border states, Ch'in had achieved great military and economic advances. How Ch'in differed was in its consistent policy of maximization of power, individual details of which resemble the measures taken in Ch'i under the ministry of Kuan Chung. The Ch'in policy is closely linked with the name of Shang Yang, a native of Wei, one of the Chin successor states, who served the prince of Ch'in as counsellor from 361 to 338. On his recommendation the mass of the population was divided into units of mutual control and responsibility and put to produce the basic products, the products, that is, of agriculture. His chief object, however, was the abolition of the powers of the hereditary aristocracy. To this end he reformed the legal system, henceforward characterized by standard rewards and penalties of universal application, and he placed the whole territory under the direct control of the prince. In the year 350 Ch'in was divided into thirty-one administrative units (*hsien*). An official (*ling*) appointed by the court was made responsible for each. The previous existence of similar units has already been mentioned in Ch'i, and they were later set up in Ch'u, too, but only in the newly conquered areas. In Ch'in the system was applied for the first time to the entire state.

Ch'in thus set up a genuine, practicable alternative to the feudal system. It was more efficient than feudalism, in respect of the growing size and differentiation of social and political institutions; it was more realistic as a means of organizing power. In the Time of the Warring States political theorists provided the policy of Shang Yang and, reaching further back, Kuan Chung, with a philosophical and theoretical justification. To begin with, as in the *Book of Master Kuan* (*Kuantzu*) and the *Book of Lord Shang* (*Shang-chün shu*), these theorizings were still very heterogeneous. But in the writings of Han Fei-tzu (d. 233 BC) they attained a stylistic clarity which matched the rationality of the new practice of power. Their central concern, as of most current schools of thought, was the defeat of chaos and the restoration of stability and security. Proceeding from the axiom formulated by his teacher, the Confucian Hsün-tzu (*c.* 300–237 BC), that man is bad by nature, Han Fei-tzu rejected moral standards (virtue) and ritual norms (loyalty) as political expedients and forms of political relationship, on the grounds that they could only be injurious to the state and government, and therefore to stability and security. Such means could only perpetuate chaos. They must be replaced by binding legal obligations, 'reward and punishment' (*shang-fa*), rigorously applied, without respect of rank and title, to every member of the state, including the prince himself. This universal application of legal penalties was a principal target for criticism from the later Confucian upper class. In their view legal penalties should apply only to the lower sectors of the population. The insistence on standard penalties on the part of this school was so emphatic that its representatives became known as 'Legalists' (*fa-chia*). They also upheld the abolition of hereditary privileges already referred to, the elimination of 'unproductive' activities such as trade and religious and philosophical occupations, the setting up of state monopolies in politically and financially important raw materials and the absolute pre-eminence of military successes. Moreover, this school of thinkers totally rejected the past as model or guide. Their orientation was in the present, their goal the shaping of the future – an almost unique instance in early Chinese history. One member of the school was Li Ssu, minister to Cheng, the Ch'in king and later emperor, from 246 to 210. Li Ssu was a native of Ch'u, and was thus a 'guest minister' or 'immigrant' (Franke/Trauzettel) like Shang Yang, and he had been a pupil of Hsün-tzu, like Han Fei-tzu. Li Ssu played a crucial part in setting up the organization of the newly united empire. Evidently he saw as his principal task the counteracting of all the centrifugal tendencies which might tear the unified state to shreds. The whole empire was administratively divided, as the Ch'in kingdom had been, into 'commands' (*chün*), subdivided into 'prefectures' (*hsien*). Two governors administered each command, a civil (*shou*) and a military (*chün-wei*). A third official (*chien-yü-shih*), was placed above these two as the immediate representative in each district of the central power. Taxes were made uniform and levied without distinctions; every subject had a theoretically equal, extremely high, burden of statute labour; measures, weights and the axles of wheeled vehicles were standardized. This last meant, in effect, a standardization of tracks. Another innovation attributed to Li Ssu was the standardization of the many different scripts. This measure, by improving the means of communication, was another that facilitated the central exercise of government. Li Ssu is also credited with the first moves towards ideological conformity among the people, in so far as they could read. In the year 213, he allegedly collected all the writings on an 'index' compiled in the light of his political ideas, and had them destroyed. They included not only the chronicles of the royal houses overthrown by the Ch'in, and the writings of idealistic thinkers like the Confucians, but also the oldest books of the Chinese tradition, such as the *Book of Documents* and the *Book of Songs*. Only 'technical and scientific' works, on agriculture, military skills, medicine and the interpretation of omens, were spared. Special measures were introduced to suppress the former hereditary aristocracy: they were forbidden to carry arms, the principal families were obliged to live in the capital city and large estates were dispersed among private individuals. This last not only meant an increase in state revenue, by removing from the land its status of exemption from taxation, but was motivated by the realization that property split up into small units loses its influence.

There was always some opposition to the Legalists' measures and their views. This was probably not least because theirs was the only school of thought towards the end of the Chou period which was politically successful. Later, when the Confucians had gained the upper hand, they were condemned as downright heretical, especially Li Ssu. Nevertheless, they had an immense subsequent influence. Even in Confucian China their methods of government continued to be used. The Legalist legacy has remained one of the most important elements of the Chinese state until the present day.

While the first Ch'in emperor lived, the empire was stable. Immediately after his death (210 BC), however, power passed into weaker hands, and its basis began to disintegrate. The accelerated development of the means of communication was of no avail. The extreme degree to which power had been centralized meant that everything depended on efficiency at the centre. This was crucially impaired by internal dissension at the Ch'in court, to which the degenerate heir of Cheng fell a victim. Also, in the provinces, so recently subdued, opposition to the regime flared up again, spearheaded by the educated and the upper classes who had been deprived of their profitable sinecures and cherished traditions. There were uprisings in every region of the empire, from which two outstanding leaders eventually emerged, Hsiang Yü from what had formerly been Ch'u, and Liu Pang from what had been Ch'i. Hsiang Yü, himself of aristocratic descent, hoped to restore the old order. He soon set about distributing his conquests among descendants of the earlier princely families, offering the title of emperor to a Ch'u prince, and reserving for himself the office of hegemon. His opponent Liu Pang, meanwhile, who had been a minor official in eastern China and was the son of farmers, pursued from the first more realistic policies, building on

77

the basis left by the Ch'in administration. He seems to have realized that the old order offered no foundation for the government of the whole empire. He gained a significant advantage over Hsiang Yü in reaching the capital city first and winning the support of a large number of experienced officials while the fighting was still going on. With the death of Hsiang Yü (206 BC), the Han dynasty founded by Liu Pang was in undisputed control of the empire.

Liu Pang's measures to stabilize his rule, legitimized by neither descent nor ideology, were pragmatic and opportunist in the extreme. The detested penal legislation of the Ch'in was at first revoked; relatives and deserving followers were rewarded with fiefs in the further corners of the empire. This partial return to a feudal organization created more problems for the central administration than it solved. The Han rulers spent nearly fifty years trying to rid themselves of the new regional princes so created, or at least to render them politically impotent. They did not succeed until 154 BC, when the seven strongest vassal kings lost all their power after a rebellion. Only from then is it strictly accurate to speak of the Han empire as a centralized state. It was still a few years before the institutions and organization necessary to maintain the central power were made so strong by the energetic and unscrupulous Emperor Wu-ti (reigned 141–87 BC) that they remained a model for centuries to come. A chancellor (ch'eng-hsiang) was placed at the head of a strong court administration, which was already rudimentarily divided into special-ized departments. All the officials in central and local administration were appointed directly by the central government. Almost the whole empire was divided into commands and prefectures. Even in the smaller fiefs that still remained, most important affairs were conducted by officials from the central government. But this system of government was intact only in the immediate vicinity of the capital. Towards the periphery regional independence steadily increased, in the form of influence wielded by the large landowners. Here the duties of the imperial officials were most likely to collide with the interests of the emperor's subjects. These duties fell broadly into two categories: preventing the large landowners from developing too much power in the provinces, and ensuring that the mass of the population paid their taxes and performed their statute labour. The welfare of the popula-tion at large was not part of the officials' duties.

Political power in traditional China was always largely a matter of economic policy, more precisely, taxation policy – not in a modern sense, however, but exclusively as a means of safeguarding and strengthening the central power. The economic policy initiated by Han Wu-ti and pursued by his successors had two basic characteristics: creaming off the maximum possible value from agricultural resources, and monopolizing all the financially and strategically important branches of production. In the year 119 BC state monopolies in salt and iron were once again proclaimed, and the production and sale of alcohol were added to them not long after. Some years later the minting of coins had been made a state monopoly (112 BC). Wu-ti and his ministers showed the greatest skill in manipulating the value of the coinage to benefit the imperial exchequer. On more than one occasion some of the coins in circulation were devalued. The emperor also issued 'loans', for which his wealthy subjects had to pay out 40,000 pieces. The sale of offices and the opportunity to pay fines in lieu of undergoing punishment were also introduced under Wu-ti. Another innovation was the attempt to profit by fluctuations in the prices of the most important mass products. The first moves were made in 110 BC to set up a system of price adjustment, whereby during good harvests, central government bought the surplus, especially of grain, cheaply, in order to resell it at higher prices when and where production was poor. The system resulted in stabilization and equability of supply, though these were not its prime purposes. These practices laid the foundations of some of the essential and traditional measures of indirect taxation. They were symptomatic of future economic policies of the Chinese state.

Conflict between the centre and the periphery was accentuated not only by the imperfections of the infrastructure and physical distance, but also by the administrative officials themselves. It was decreed in 134 BC that each prefecture should annually nominate a specific number of potential officials. Moreover, every official from the rank of prefect upwards and with at least three years of service to his credit was given the right to propose a son or brother as candidate. The essential quality required of would-be civil servants was 'aptitude', of which a candidate's promoter was expected to provide guarantees. This gave rise to the vicious circle, already referred to, of wealth-education-wealth. At first it favoured the individual parties more than the central government. The foundation in 124 BC of a state academy for the training of officials at imperial expense was a preliminary attempt to counteract that trend. This first move to enable the central government to select and educate its agents was modest and inadequate

79

in itself, but it was the start of the Confucian specialization and monopoly in the education of the Chinese civil service. From these modest beginnings arose the examination system so characteristic of later Chinese life. Also, and above all, there developed the convergence between the interests of the head of state and of the civil service, which led to the problematic identity of Confucianism with the monarchy.

It may seem surprising that Confucianism, while failing since its inception to gain any noteworthy direct political influence, was suddenly able to take over a totally Legalist system of government without any apparent intermediate stages. The development was not, in fact, all that surprising, as a short survey of the evolution of Confucianism will reveal.

Confucius (*c.* 551–497 BC) succeeded in founding a rational, personal ethic and morality on the traditional rites (*li*) and the magical, mystical force of virtue (*te*). He addressed himself primarily to the nobility, seeking reforms in them that would stabilize the crumbling society of his day. At the heart of his teaching lay moral fitness and legitimacy, qualities that could not be inherited, in his view, but could and must be learned. The object of his concern was the social world, in which alone man could fully realize himself and fulfil his destiny. Confucius founded a social ethic and an agnostic tradition which retained their pre-eminence in spite of speculative accretions at later dates. Characteristically, Confucius did not, like many later 'Confucians', project the existing social order on to the universe, as a means of justifying that order: the order of his day was too unsatisfactory for that. Back projection of that kind is typical of a complacent society. Confucius, on the contrary, constructed a Utopia, which he projected back into the past. He never significantly influenced anyone holding power in his lifetime. But his ideas were handed on and, as time went by, were discussed, adopted, rejected and adopted again. The best known of his followers in the latter part of the Chou era were Meng-tzu (Mencius) (371–289 BC) and Hsün-tzu (*c.* 300–237 BC). Meng-tzu made the legitimacy of a ruler dependent on the acceptance of the entire people, rather than on any personal claims. He placed the people at the head of his scale of values, instead of the 'gentleman' (*chün-tzu*). His basic premiss was that all men were equally morally good by nature, and that this innate morality could and should be nurtured by constant attention. The 'royal path' (*wang-tao*) did not consist of imposing government by force but of winning men's allegiance by 'humanity' (*jen*). In Meng-tzu's scheme of things, the people were the instrument of heaven. If a ruler failed and was deposed by his people, heaven withdrew its mandate from him (*ko-ming*: the modern meaning of this expression is revolution). Disobedience and rebellion were fully justified in Meng-tzu's view, provided they were successful. Hsün-tzu's initial premiss was diametrically opposed to Meng-tzu's: man, the offshoot of an impersonal, immoral Nature, driven by his passions and emotions, was basically bad. Only education and training could make a 'social' being out of him. Rites and ceremonials would play a decisive part in the appropriate kind of education. Hsün-tzu was in favour of hierarchic order and a rigid class system. He believed that the world would be ordered perfectly adequately by means of discipline at every level, punishment and the threat of punishment. Of all the Confucian philosophers of the pre-Han era, Hsün-tzu probably had the greatest political influence. This was partly because his school led on to the most successful theorists of the age, the Legalists, and partly because his adaptation of earlier Confucian thought prepared it for transference to a Legalist basis. The Confucian tradition, like most others, was proscribed under the Ch'in. In the early decades of Han rule nothing indicated its revival. Yet gradually thinkers of the most widely varying persuasions began to identify themselves with the Confucian tradition. It seems that, in spite of the interruption of the tradition and its lack of practical success, Confucianism had retained its high reputation. At all events, from the early Han period onwards Confucius was again accorded the greatest respect. By the time Confucianism became state dogma under Han Wu-ti, it had developed into a syncretic mixture of the most heterogeneous elements, hardly deserving the name of Confucian, less a system of ethics than cosmological speculation compounded with utilitarian prognostics. It has been said that the 'Confucians' did nothing except what the emperor required (Ku Chieh-kang). The new Confucianism was definitively formulated by Tung Chung-shu (*c.* 171–104 BC), at whose instigation the first state examinations were introduced. He managed not only to equate law and religious custom, but also to reconcile, to a certain degree, the Legalist principles of political centralization and functionalism with the feudal and moral principles of Confucius. Similarly, Tung Chung-shu married the Confucian and Legalist elements of his teaching with the Nature philosophy of the Yin and Yang school, as well as with an interpretation of the omens he found in the *Spring and Autumn Annals*

81

ascribed to Confucius. He thus arrived at a comprehensive historico-prognostic panorama of both past and future. The legitimacy of the Han dynasty was one of the things Tung Chung-shu sought to sanction by this means. Even in the Han period voices were raised against such historico-political determinism, though to no avail. The symbiosis of Legalism and Confucianism that took place in the reign of Han Wu-ti under these auspices remained characteristic of the Chinese empire until its very end. It was due to one cause, over and above the personalities and the personal factors already mentioned, namely that in its transformed shape Confucianism proved to be the only political theory, favourable to supremacism and imperialism, that could mediate between centripetal and centrifugal tendencies within the empire. This Confucianism offered not so much a prescription for fashioning the world, as a most exhaustive interpretation and justification of a strong central ruler. Later Confucians regretted and criticized such a development. In the eyes of the great philosopher Huang Tsung-hsi (1610–95), 'pure' Confucian thought had been continuously falsified in favour of 'despotic' Confucianism, i.e. Legalism, ever since the foundation of the empire under the Ch'in dynasty. In fact, both contributed to form the centralized, unified state of China. Without the Legalist basis the Confucian superstructure would have been unable to develop.

After, and partly during, the reign of Han Wu-ti, changes occurred once more in the provinces that did not suit the central power. The rich landowners, who were taxed leniently or even exempted for services to the state, added substantially to their property at the expense of the small farmers. This amassment of lands and men – the farmers who sold out generally remained on their former plots, to work them for the new owners – greatly diminished the revenue from taxation. It also produced deficiencies in statute labour that had to be made good by the remaining independent small farmers who were not exempted from these obligations. While the situation worsened for the central government, and as other factors threatened the dynasty towards the end of the first century BC, an attempt at intervention was made by Wang Mang, known as the Usurper. Wang Mang was a nephew of the empress, and had acted as regent in the years AD 1 to 8, while the emperor was a boy. He systematically used omens to convince the court that the only means of salvaging the situation was to depose the young emperor and establish a new dynasty – to be called 'New [Dynasty]'. In this way he succeeded in placing himself at the head of the state without the use of force. This was largely due to the role in the state ideology of prognostication and the interpretation of omens. Straightaway, in AD 9, he ordered the dissolution of the large, tax-exempt estates, to be redistributed among small, tax-paying farmers. This measure was accompanied by a series of other decrees, all intended to strengthen the central authority, such as a ban on private ownership of slaves. Understandably, Wang Mang immediately fell foul of the particularist interests of the wealthy families who had not been effectively made powerless. Several revolts broke out, which at first achieved little. Only in AD 18 did the anti-centre movement gain momentum. In this year, farmers, especially in the eastern part of Shantung, uprooted by floods and general chaos resulting from an alteration in the course of the Huangho, began to band together, using such names as the 'Red Eyebrows'. Wang Mang was killed in the year 23 by rebels, by that time led by representatives of the very groups which, having successfully undermined the power of the central government, now aspired to take it for themselves.

It finally fell to a scion of the Han called Liu Hsiu (reigned as Han Kuang-wu AD 25–27), who had been a well-to-do landowner on the Huangho plains, to eliminate most of the rival claimants to the imperial throne. Since he was a Han and claimed to be restoring the Han dynasty, he met with hardly any opposition, once he had proved himself a strong man. A large number of the privileged families having disappeared in the course of the disturbances, Kuang-wu was able for the time, to re-establish the central power, within limits. But neither politically nor economically and financially were the later Han able to regain the level of their dynastic predecessors. The structure of society remained virtually unchanged. In north China in particular, the catchment area closest to the seat of the central government, the concentration of tax-exempt and tax-privileged estates proceeded apace. Large sectors of the population fled the growing burden of taxation and statute labour, imposed upon them by the great landowners. Most migrated to the thinly populated south. The farmers who became tenants of the privileged landowners had to hand over to them about half their produce and become available for domestic service. The landlords, for their part, paid in taxes, if anything at all, perhaps a thirtieth of their income. The profits of the tenants' labours thus went almost entirely to the landlords. They then re-invested them in yet more land and so depleted the sources of state revenue even further. Alternatively they used them to manipulate civil servants, whether

83

their kinsmen or not, in order politically to safeguard their own position. The emperor was boycotted by the wealthy and the privileged, prominent among whom were the families of successive empresses. The later Han emperors were mostly weaklings increasingly dependent on their eunuchs for help in containing the growing power of their in-laws, and in controlling the families of the landowning and administrative class in the vicinity of the capital. From the second century onwards the eunuchs on the one hand and the emperors' unloving relations and the power-hungry 'clans of academicians' on the other were clearly in conflict. Several exterminatory campaigns made the eunuchs' position so secure that they themselves became a serious threat to the court. But their influence was on the whole restricted to the court and the vicinity of the capital.

Towards the end of the second century a new series of uprisings began (the Yellow Turbans). It was at this time neither the eunuchs, the imperial kinsmen, nor the 'academicians' who dictated the course of events, but essentially three generals, all members of wealthy landowning families. As taxable resources had dwindled, the system of statute labour, and thus also the reservoir for the imperial army, had declined. The emperor was obliged to turn to certain landowners who had built up their own domestic armies (*pu-ch'ü*). At first it seemed these private generals would support the dynasty. Before long, however, the court found itself in a state of siege. At the beginning of the third century the emperor was left with neither power nor authority. In the year 220 the throne was seized by Ts'ao P'ei (187–226), son and successor of Ts'ao Ts'ao (155–220), the commander of a private army who had been all-powerful in north China for a generation, and the Wei dynasty was proclaimed. Ts'ao P'ei justified his action by reference to the legendary kings Yao and Shun, who had come to the throne by other than patrilinear succession. A year later another general, Liu Pei (161–223), proclaimed the foundation of his dynasty, the Shu, also known as Han Shu on the grounds of Liu Pei's distant family connection with the Han. Liu Pei's realm consisted essentially only of the further Ssechuan basin. Lastly, in 222 a third powerful general, Sun Ch'üan (182–252), who controlled the middle and lower Yangtse valley and the regions to the south of it, claimed the title of emperor. He called his dynasty Wu, after the state that had existed in his territory at the time of the Chou. The period of the 'Three Kingdoms' had begun.

The centralized Han state had fallen into three distinct parts which have been defined as 'key economic regions' (Chi Ch'ao-ting). Within these, separate political groupings and centres of gravity were to form and re-form time and again. The three areas were distinguished above all by their demographic and economic structures. The Huangho plain, including the Shensi basin and the Shansi highlands, was still the most important region, economically and demographically. By comparison, the middle and lower Yangtse valley and the further Ssechuan basin were in a colonial state, sparsely populated and economically still expanding and extending. Several factors had contributed to the collapse of the centralized state. Central among them was the tension between the centre and the periphery. This was manifested in the conflict between the central ruler's claim to total power, while attempting to control the empire indirectly and impersonally through officials, and the particularist interests of the great privileged landowners. This tension only profited the centre while a strong emperor headed the government. Otherwise the empire's organization, infrastructure and social structure were still inadequate to sustain in the long term a large centralized state. This is well illustrated by the short-lived Chin dynasty, which succeeded in uniting the empire again for a few decades before it split up into more than a dozen small states, some of extremely short duration, existing simultaneously or rapidly succeeding each other. Some of these states were little more than large family alliances, declaring dynastic independence on the grounds of their economic autarky and exercising direct rule over their subjects by means of their numerous retainers, in a relatively small, confined economic region. Others remained dependent on the good will of powerful landowners, exactly like the Han emperors. This splintering of power went on for nearly three centuries. A constant characteristic of the period was the broad division of the whole Chinese area into the 'Chinese' states in the south, that is, those that claimed to resemble the Han regime, and the 'barbarian' dynasties in the north. It was the time of the 'Southern and Northern Dynasties'. Individual rulers repeatedly tried to overcome the excessive diffusion of power, which even extended to the great domains within the separate states. The Equal Field System (chün-t'ien) played an important part in this situation. Despite various attempted methods of implementation, the system remained on the whole an ideal vainly striven for by pretenders to the central power. It had already been tried by the Chin in one form, and provided for the distribution of land, except that given as fiefs to supporters and kinsmen, among all male

85

adults, under the Chin those between the ages of sixteen and sixty. It was undermined, not only by the inadequacy of the administrative apparatus necessary to cope with the constant changes of ownership, but also by the very officials who were supposed to administer it, and who also received a specific portion of the land, according to their rank. Theoretically they were not allowed to increase their holdings above the fixed amount. But the chronic weakness of the princes calling themselves emperor meant that in practice the limits were ignored. The lack of any material basis was not the least of the reasons for their weakness. The dilemma was typical of many periods of later Chinese history, but it was never so pronounced as in these years of scission. In brief, neither of the two essential prerequisites for effective centralization of power – substantial revenues from taxation and a loyal civil service – existed in anything like an adequate form. A reduction of privileges would have deprived the ruler of the coopera-tion of his officials; dispensing with officials would have deprived him of the means to rule. The situation can best be described as a variable stalemate. It was particularly acute in south China.

It was not one of the southern states that succeeded in re-unifying the empire, but a dynasty from the 'barbarian' north. Since the third century, the north had been invaded by a large number of alien tribes. Often these were no more than small groups of warriors: proto-Mongolian Hsien-pi, Turkish Hsiung-nu and Chieh, Tibetan Ti and Ch'iang, to name only a few. They all founded separate states, more or less on the Chinese model, though without copying the machinery of government and administration developed to the last detail under the Han emperors. The Toba, a branch of the Hsien-pi, seem an excep-tion. In 386 they adopted the Chinese dynastic name of Northern Wei. By about the middle of the fifth century they had ousted their non-Chinese rivals and possessed all north China. Unlike the other con-tenders they distributed only a very small amount of their conquests among their own people. The rest they exploited for themselves by means of a traditional Chinese administration. Emperor Hsiao-wen (reigned 471–99), for instance, developed the Equal Field System by an expedient division of the land into 'permanent holdings' (*yung-yeh*), which could be passed on by inheritance, and 'poll shares' (*k'ou-fen*), of which the tenant enjoyed the usufruct. Hsiao-wen also pursued a systematic sinization of the Toba. Chinese was the only language allowed at court; all the Toba were ordered to wear Chinese dress and have Chinese names; and they were encouraged to intermarry with ethnic Chinese. Understandably these measures met with opposition within the Toba ranks themselves. There was also friction between the foreign warriors and the Chinese administrators. The sharp division between the civil and the military arms, later so typical of China, probably began under the Toba, who found it expedient to use Chinese officials in the civil sphere but not in the military. The later contempt for the military as a profession fit for barbarians would have had a very solid foundation in such a context.

The Wei court lost its pre-eminence, and the Toba-Wei were eventually replaced by three small new dynasties, of whom the Northern Chou deserve special mention. From their seat in the Shensi and Kansu basins they contrived, in 577, to re-unite the whole of the north. They also produced the man who finally brought the whole of China together under one central rule again after nearly three hundred years, Yang Chien (541–604). He came to the fore as commander of the Northern Chou army and in 581 he seized their throne for himself. He at once proclaimed a new dynasty, to which he gave the name of Sui. It is not clear whether he was of Chinese or Toba descent. He probably belonged, like many of his contemporaries, to the new race resulting from the miscegenation of Chinese and aliens in north China over several centuries.

Once the Sui had taken the last separate southern state, Ch'en, in 589, they tried, much like the Ch'in, to consolidate their power too quickly and too rigorously. True, maybe no other course lay open to them, after the empire had been in pieces for nearly three centuries. The desire for unity may well have been widespread, but hardly any of the rulers of the little states was prepared to accept it at the expense of his own independence. The moves made to strengthen the central power were therefore mostly concerned with internal stabilization. The expansionist thrusts into the world outside, on the other hand, were aggressive rather than defensive. The second Sui emperor, Yang-ti (reigned 605–18), later vilified as a notorious scoundrel, was at first particularly successful at unification. To win over the ruling circles in the south, who were adherents of Buddhism, he showed favour to Buddhist organizations, especially the T'ien-t'ai sect. He furthered the consistent application of the Equal Field System in regions depopulated and left uncultivated as a result of the civil wars. By extending the Imperial Canal, the *yün-ho*, linking the Che River and the Huangho, he improved communications between the demographic and political centre in the north and the area of economic expansion in the south. The work involved the mobilization of over a million forced labourers, hundreds of thousands of whom allegedly died in the swamps or through exhaustion. The burdens and constraints piled upon the people and the upper classes were such that at the very time of Yang-ti's defeats in his Korean campaigns (612–14), he also faced open rebellion at home. He was thereafter on the defensive, and was assassinated in the south in 618.

It is significant that the Sui, like the Ch'in, were not able to stay in power at the head of the empire for very long, after it had been reunited for the first time for centuries. After both long periods of polycentralism, strong anti-central tendencies operated for at least a generation, erupting virulently at the first moment of weakness on the part of the central power. In both cases it proved possible to halt the process. The empire did not break up again after the fall of the Sui. One of their officials, an aristocrat called Li Yüan (566–635), who claimed Chinese ancestry, like the Sui themselves, rose against them in 617, and with the help of Turkish allies took the capital Ch'ang-an. A year later he there proclaimed the T'ang dynasty. Li Yüan, posthumously named Kao-tsu, was supported, indeed apparently driven, in his bid for power by his ambitious son Li Shih-min, posthumously named T'ai-tsung (reigned 626–49). After eliminating his brothers, Li Shih-min made his father abdicate in his favour (626). He continued the forays into the territories outside China begun by the Sui. His power still rested on a dynamic, military basis. As under the Han emperors, expansion of the empire had a significant internal effect. The burden it placed on the state was offset by acquisition of immense areas into which the nation could spread at a time of decisive growth, so helping to neutralize social tensions. Meanwhile the central government's security rested less on external successes than on internal political and fiscal organization. The new regime was able to carry on directly with the system of taxation and economics left by the Toba-Wei and the Sui; but there remained little of which it could make political and administrative use. The southern states had by and large been aristocracies, which it was impossible for a central power to take over unchanged; the northern states had been ruled by a centralized military government, more or less successfully. The T'ang system was therefore a revival and development of the organization that had existed under the Han. It was clearly intended to create an equilibrium between the various groups who held power, so that none of them endangered the central authority. The exercise of power was sectionalized from the very top. Two organs of central government were functionally very close to the emperor, but each acted as a control on the other. They were the Imperial Secretariat (*chung-shu-sheng*), responsible for drafting the imperial edicts, and thus for political statements of all kinds – the Historiographical Office (*shih-kuan*) also belonged to it – and the Chancellory (*men-hsia-sheng*), where all petitions were first studied and the edicts drafted by the Secretariat were read through and referred back if not approved. The third of the three primary organs of the central administration (*san-sheng*) was the State Chancellory (*shang-shu-sheng*). This carried out instructions agreed on by the first two, through the agency of six subordinate ministries (*liu-pu*). These were the Civil Service Ministry (*li-pu*), the Finance Ministry (*hu-pu*), the Ministry of Ceremonies. (*li-pu*), the Army Ministry (*ping-pu*), the Justice Ministry (*hsing-pu*) and the Ministry of Public Works (*kung-pu*). All the offices of these ministries and of the regional administration were under the supervision of the Censorate (*yü-shih-t'ai*), whose staff made their reports directly to the emperor himself. Their duties included checking on the ideological reliability of civil servants. In the sphere of local government, the T'ang took over the machinery set up by the Sui. The whole empire was divided into 'prefectures' (*chou*) and 'subprefectures' (*hsien*), but a new, larger unit, called a circuit (*tao*), was inserted at regional level, the precursor of the later province. The capital was linked to the distant centres of administration by a radial network of posting stations, complete with rest-houses and facilities for changing horses or boats. The border regions were administered by military authorities, 'general governorships' (*tu-tu-fu*) and 'general protectorates' (*tu-hu-fu*). Civil servants in these regions were subordinate to the commanding general.

Most of the many officials required to run this governmental apparatus had passed the state examinations re-introduced under the Sui. As in the Han period, Confucian teachings were central to the curriculum. Uniformity of training and selection gradually produced a civil service that was both ideologically reliable and largely homogeneous. Up to the eighth century, however, it was still dominated by the powerful families, some still aristocratic, who controlled the Civil Service Ministry that ran the state examinations, and who therefore held a monopoly in the distribution of profitable offices. Thereafter, responsibility for the examinations went to the Ministry of Ceremonies, which otherwise supervised Confucian rites and official ceremonial,

89

including diplomatic protocol. The Civil Service Ministry, meanwhile, continued to assign the successful candidates to their grades and posts. Thus recruitment at least became more objective. On the other hand, the absolutism of the emperor grew in proportion as the aristocracy's power to perpetuate their privileges dwindled, and as examination success and civil service careers became the norm for the acquisition of wealth and membership of the upper classes.

Towards the end of the seventh century, not for the first time, nor the last, an empress gained control of the government. After several years as *de facto* ruler, on behalf of two weakling sons, the widow of the third T'ang emperor, Empress Wu (625–705), seized the throne itself in 690 and proclaimed herself the first emperor of a new Chou dynasty. In that respect the case was unique in Chinese history. Only in 705 could the empress, by then eighty years old, be deposed. A similar attempt by another imperial consort and her family was only prevented by the annihilation of the whole clan. The frequency of these attempts shows that, in the governing classes at least, a woman was more loyal to her own family than to her husband's. Empress Wu was the daughter of a rich merchant and had been brought up a strict Buddhist. During her reign, however, she did her best to encourage not only Buddhism but also Taoism and Confucianism. It was under her that the syncretic religion took shape which was later interpreted as a unitary religion (*han san wei i*), Chinese 'universism' as de Groot called it. Buddhism, which came to China in the first century AD, became widespread in the centuries when the empire was divided between the Han and the T'ang. During this time it acquired many specifically Chinese characteristics. Taoism also gained many adherents in the same period. Both doctrines fostered each other, although they sometimes also clashed. Buddhism benefited from the receptivity prepared in the Chinese by Taoism; Taoism adopted from Buddhism organizational forms which strengthened its worldly position. The success they both enjoyed, particularly Buddhism, coming as it did from outside China, cannot be attributed to the stimulus of their conflict of ideas so much as to the historical situation following the collapse of the Han dynasty. Both can be described as religions of refuge, which met people's needs, not least those of the upper classes, to whom, even more than to the masses, the world must have seemed to be sliding down into chaos. The worldly doctrines of the Legalist brand of Confucianism appeared to have failed them. Taoism and Buddhism not only offered interpretations of the world that went

90

beyond the limits of Confucianism, but also showed ways of escaping from the ruined world. Confucianism had defined the position of man in an ordered society; Taoism explained man's relationship to the entire universe; Buddhism showed man a path of individual redemption, even of release from the universe altogether. Taoism and Buddhism found the utmost encouragement and support in very nearly all the separate states. The Toba-Wei even adopted Buddhism as the state religion. By the time the empire was re-united the various temples, monasteries and sects were well-established, strong and privileged. They continued developing almost without interference in the first half of the T'ang period. In so doing they helped to undermine the central power, for their privileges enabled some monasteries, especially Buddhist ones, like the great Catholic houses of medieval Europe, to accumulate immense estates, engage in trade and become financiers on a grand scale. Only under the T'ang emperors was the temporal power in China confronted by a genuine ecclesiastical organization. Characteristically, the rivalry reached its climax in economic affairs.

But the monasteries were not the only threat to the central power. Under the T'ang, as almost always before, the Equal Field System had led only to temporary and local stabilization of property holdings and hence of taxation revenue. The preferential rights of civil servants and their families and of the nobility permitted large estates to be accumulated legally. There were, additionally, illegal methods, such as falsifying the registers and privately appropriating the properties of small farmers who had got into debt. The greatest evil of the socio-economic structure, the amassment of property by a privileged class, was as rife as ever before. It did not merely symptomize social injustice; it also endangered the central power. Furthermore, from the early eighth century, the civil administration throughout the empire was gradually overlaid by a military administration. Within this system, district 'commanders' (*chieh-tu-shih*) held permanent appointments, and were acknowledged as the direct representatives of the emperor. They had professional soldiers under their command, and were completely free to dispose of the produce of their own districts. These commands were instituted to strengthen the central power, by countering centrifugal tendencies in the empire. It soon emerged, however, that they were more prone to independence than any other branch of government. This is the background to the reign of Emperor Hsüan-tsung (reigned 713–56), often celebrated as the most brilliant

of the T'ang rulers on account of the artistic and intellectual efflorescence of his time. While the T'ang empire undoubtedly appeared
the largest, richest and best-ordered country in the Far East, and
perhaps in the whole world, at that date, the process of decline was
already under way. In 755 the military commander of three frontier
districts, An Lu-shan (693–757), racially a non-Chinese, rose in
rebellion. He conquered the two capital cities of Lo-yang and Ch'ang-
an in quick succession, and in 756 proclaimed his own Yen dynasty.
He was assassinated a year later by his son. But not until 763 did the
T'ang disperse the immediate threat, with the help of foreign troops.
The military commanders were beyond their control. By the end of
the eighth century the commands were being passed from father to
son in every part of the empire. A carving-up process was beginning.
The central government did not yield readily. Numerous measures
were introduced to overcome the financial crisis. The salt monopoly
was re-imposed even before the An Lu-shan rebellion had been completely put down (758). The alcohol monopoly (782) and the tea
monopoly (793) followed before the end of the century. In 780 the
Double Tax System (*liang-shui fa*) was introduced, which simplified
and improved collection, but also took into account the realities of
ownership of property. The new system was by no means just, but
with the passage of time, which in China often means the passage of
centuries, it changed the fundamental socio-economic structure. From
that date on taxes were no longer levied *per capita*, but on land.
The result was a relatively equalized burden. Moreover, rich landowners were no longer quasi-aristocrats, with estates virtually exempt
from taxation, but landlords liable to tax. Another fiscal innovation
took the form of the campaigns to secularize and dispossess the great
monasteries and bring large parts of their estates back into production
(842–45). All these measures had a lasting effect. The nobility and
organized Buddhism lost their privileged positions, and never played
a decisive role again. But the variable equilibrium formerly existing
between the imperial family, the aristocracy, the quasi-aristocratic
landowners and the military commanders changed not in favour of
the emperor, but of the generals, some of whom had begun to fight
for mastery towards the end of the ninth century. The officials who
had risen through the examination system were not currently equal to
an independent part in the struggle.

The struggle erupted openly with a popular insurrection headed by
a failed examination candidate, Huang Ch'ao. Chu Wen (852–912),

a military commander who had at first fought against the T'ang, but then joined them, emerged as the victor. In 907 he founded his own dynasty, the Later Liang. It was the first of the five extremely short-lived attempts to establish dynasties in north China, which gave this period in Chinese history the name of the 'Five Dynasties'. At the same time, in the south and west there were the 'Ten Kingdoms' (*shih-kuo*), some of whose rulers also claimed the title of emperor. None the less, events differed from those following the collapse of the Han. Principally, the empire was divided during a much shorter time, so that regional differences hardly had time to develop. It was also significant that there were fewer foreign influences or invasions in this period. The only invaders who left any enduring traces were the Kitan, a semi-nomad people of Mongolian descent. They founded a dynasty on the Chinese model, the Liao, in 946, in the Liao lowlands in southern Manchuria.

When one of the five north Chinese pretenders to the throne fell during a campaign against the Kitan-Liao, a general, Chao Kuang-yin (927–76), assumed command. His election as emperor in 960 was at least in part his own doing. He called his dynasty Sung, and under it China was once more re-united. No clear principal reason exists for the relative speed with which it came under a central authority again. Certainly it was important that the Later Han dynasty, one of the five northern states, had restricted the power of the military and subdued them to the authority of the prince in that state by appointing 'control commissioners' (*hsün-chien-shih*). But even more important was perhaps that the sense of belonging to a united state had had a long time to take root in the Chinese heartland. In the light of her later history, it can be said that by that time China had become a virtually indestructible political unit, still capable of division, but only for very short periods. Particularist ambitions on the periphery would continue to endanger dynasties in the future. But to the empire itself they could only be a temporary hazard. Some Chinese historians, incidentally, nowadays postulate the integrity of the empire as characteristic of the entire course of Chinese history (Ch'ien Mu).

Like the founders of other dynasties, Chao Kuang-yin, whose dynastic title was T'ai-tsu (reigned 960–76), set the tone of his dynasty's character. He skilfully put paid to the most immediate danger, the unlimited independence of the regional military commanders, who had been decisive in the fall of the T'ang and the division of the empire. He assembled the best troops in the vicinity of the capital and put

93

them under the direct command of a civil body, the Privy State Council (*shu-mi-yüan*). He retired most of his own generals with generous pensions. The remaining military commanders were left with only a prefecture each and as they died off they were replaced by civilian officials. At the same time T'ai-tsu and his successors sought to strengthen themselves through the administrative organization. They retained the T'ang structure in its essentials, but the central government was brought more effectively under the personal control of the emperor. The function of the various chancellors (*tsai-hsiang*), who had enjoyed a large degree of independence under the T'ang, was now more advisory. The Secretariat-Chancellory (*chung-shu men-hsia-sheng*), responsible for the civil administration, and the Privy State Council (*shu-mi-yüan*), in charge of military affairs, were the most important of the three primary organs of government (*san-ssu*). The third specialized in financial and economic affairs. All three were headed and run by professional civil servants. The restructuring that gave the civil service pre-eminence was paralleled by extensions in recruitment and increasing insistence on formal qualifications. Means of rising remained other than the examination system, but the circle of those who achieved office by such means was relatively restricted. And by now the officials who had graduated from the state academy enjoyed a far higher prestige. From 1067 onwards the state examinations for the civil service took place in a regular three-year cycle. There were three grades of examination: prefecture, capital and palace. Ten per cent of candidates, on average, passed each stage. One noteworthy regulation related to candidates who had reached an advanced age through repeated failure: they were admitted to the service after passing a simplified examination. The regulation was probably intended both to reward their persistence and to forestall disaffection against the state. The case of the frustrated mature student Huang Ch'ao, who had headed a rebellion at the end of the T'ang regime, had probably indicated a potential source of danger to the central power. But the Sung had learned other lessons from the past, besides how to deal with generals and examination failers. They took steps to prevent concentrations of power on the peripheries of the empire by forbidding civil servants who were related by blood or marriage to serve together, and by debarring relatives of the imperial wives from high office. All these measures proved lastingly effective. Never again did a general in the imperial army, a high-ranking official or a kinsman of an empress or imperial concubine succeed in seizing the throne.

The centralization of power and with it the stability of the empire were substantially improved under the Sung emperors. Improved administrative efficiency was not the only cause: developments in the internal economic structure also played a role. Under the Sung the different regions became noticeably more dependent on each other. The traditional regional self-sufficiency of earlier centuries gave place to a comparatively complex economic structure of regional interdependence. This was so not only with specialized products and luxury goods, but also with staples such as sugar and rice. Such a development is not the least of the reasons why the Sung period is often hailed as 'modern'.

There were innovations in the conduct of political affairs, too; the struggle for power became more intellectual and programmatic. Generally, even in the dynasties following the Sung, only members of the imperial family actually attempted to seize the throne. Pressure groups and factions, as well as individual civil servants, vied to gain the emperor's ear, both to pursue particular political, economic or military policies, and in regional or personal interests. The crucial change was that the emperor, however weak, was now the fountainhead of all power. The academic civil service, dependent on this power, had visibly replaced the largely independent aristocratic and quasi-aristocratic upper classes in the Sung period. As offices and possessions became dependent on the central power alone, so the periphery was bound more firmly to the centre. But these bonds appeared only to relax the tension between the two. Particularist interests threatened the central power even under the Sung emperors. Wang An-shih (1021–86), who served the young Emperor Shen-tsung (reigned 1068–85) as chancellor from 1069 to 1076, was one of those who introduced extensive reforms to counteract these debilitating influences. Although these measures were conceived solely to strengthen the central power, like the reforms of Wang Mang they had an indirect social outcome. Wang An-shih legislated to restore justice in matters of taxation and labour; he laid down regulations for the strict supervision of trade and of fluctuations in ownership of land. These reforms affected the new upper class, of which he was a member, as much as anybody. To optimize of the civil service, he tried to improve the professional training and introduced subjects such as jurisdiction, economics, administrative geography and military studies into the examination syllabus. These subjects, recalling the priorities of the old Legalist outlook under the Ch'in emperors, contrast diametrically

95

with the abstract, moral and ethical preoccupations of the Confucian education and examination systems. A whole phalanx of conservative colleagues bitterly opposed Wang An-shih and eventually re-introduced the old *status quo*, after years of struggle. His reforms undoubtedly accorded with contemporary needs more than the ideas of his opponents; despite their short life they did constitute one more step towards long-term consolidation of the central power. Significantly, the Northern Sung were finally weakened less by peripheral pressures – although notorious economic injustices continued – than by political disagreements at the centre itself. These so weakened the bureaucratic structure that effective government became impossible. Amid these circumstances uprisings in the south (Fang La) and military setbacks in the north shook the Sung state to its very foundations.

In the first half of the eleventh century the Sung had made a very delicately balanced peace treaty with the Kitan-Liao in the north and the Tibetan-Chinese Hsi-Hsia dynasty, who had established themselves in the further Ordos region. At the beginning of the twelfth century the Sung thought they had a chance of annulling the agreement, which they found both dishonourable and economically irksome, by inflicting military defeat on the first of the other two parties to it with the help of another neighbouring race. The attack itself succeeded (1125), but a new enemy immediately confronted the Sung: their ally, the Jurchen Tungus, who had founded a dynasty of their own called Chin (1115). They penetrated the Sung empire in a series of rapid attacks, took the capital Pien (Kaifeng, Honan) in 1126, and captured the emperor. A son of the previous emperor managed to halt the advance of the Jurchen-Chin north of the Yangtse line. He carried on the Sung dynasty as Emperor Kao-tsung (reigned 1127–62) and set up his nominally 'temporary' capital (*hsing-tsai*), in Lin-an (Hangchou, Chekiang) in 1138. It is astonishing how the Sung succeeded in consolidating their power yet again. Their legitimacy was undisputed, their economic position, for the time being, strong. For the first time, the new upper class proved a stabilizing factor. Some, having followed the emperor from the north, were therefore dependent on his success; others supported the emperor because they lived in the south and sought through him to maintain their possessions and influence. The Southern Sung dynasty endured for over 150 years. It headed a state that can be described in every respect – economic vigour, intellectual sophistication, social distinctions and political rationality – as flourishing. During this period an intellectual development took place which was to have a long-term influence on political evolution, not only in China, but also in Japan, Korea and Annam.

This development was the next great change in Confucianism, following its first transformation in the Han era. It was not the work of one man alone, but the name of Chu Hsi (1130–1200) so over-shadowed all others that it was for a time synonymous with Neo-Confucianism. This was a synthesis of traditional Confucian, Buddhist and Taoist thought. It attempted a 'Confucian' interpretation of man's place in an order beyond the material world. Simultaneously, it sought to restore the 'purity' of Confucius's original teaching, especially in the field of ethics. Chu Hsi's contribution was to revive a Confucian scale of ethical values for life in the social context. The state and society became the focal centres once more. Confucianism was thus adapted to transcendental needs. In this way its influence was extended over a wider range of people; at the same time its role as the ideology of the governing power was reinforced rather than diluted. It is true that Neo-Confucianism in the form Chu Hsi gave it was by no means a political doctrine to begin with, but it became one under the Ming dynasty, and remained so until the end of the monarchy.

Politics were dominated in the twelfth and early thirteenth centuries by the differences between two parties, 'revanchists' and 'relinquishers', and by the seesawing of their influence at the court. Although the militant party was sometimes uppermost, whose aims included strengthening the military commanders and restoring their great freedom of action taken away since the T'ang period, the court and the provinces remained in civilian control. While this hindered the growth of peripheral power, the centre was embarrassed through the tax evasions of the large landowners, which even the Southern Sung emperors could not eliminate. The position was worsened by an unstable money market. Large quantities of paper money were in circulation already under the Northern Sung. Under the Southern Sung stagnation and dwindling of taxation revenue and the growing demands of military needs and treaty obligations increased the issues at an ever greater rate. The statesman Chia Ssu-tao (1213–75) attempted to halt this trend in 1263–64. With the emperor's consent he partially sequestered the possessions of some of the large estates, in the fertile regions of the south. Each landowner had to sell to the state a third of all the land he possessed above a specific minimum. He was paid with tax vouchers, patents of office and silver or paper currency. These measures, which have a Legalist smack about them, were financially successful, but

97

aggravated the latent opposition between the centre and the periphery of power. Again it was made clear that the emperor could not both acquire the fortunes of the wealthy elite, by now largely also the educational elite, while also commanding their loyalty. Chia Ssu-tao took comparable steps against the military commanders, subjecting their accounts to repeated audits, thus effectively seizing part of their property and doing nothing to strengthen their loyalty to the crown.

Thus internal tensions again perilously weakened the Sung state without a pretender rising within the state to exploit the weakness and seize power for himself. The Sung and the Ming were the only major dynasties overthrown neither by a rebel leader from the ranks, nor by a disaffected noble, but by a foreign invasion.

During the long years in which the balance of power within the geographical limits of China was more or less stabilized between the three states (Sung, Chin and Hsi-Hsia), a force grew up just outside those limits, on the steppes of Mongolia, that was to be a far greater menace to the Sung than the Kitan and the Jurchen. Historians do not fully agree even now as to how it happened. The hypothesis is disputed that the Mongols were driven to wars of aggression by the growing aridity of their homeland. Another, less historically specific explanation is that fully nomadic races regularly suffered from fluctuating resources, and that through strategic superiority the moment the neighbouring settled races weakened they easily overran them. For the Mongols, the decisive factor may very well have been the success of a few of their leaders in uniting the loose-knit tribal structure in a powerful federation. One of these leaders was Temuchin (c. 1155–1227). He took the name of Jenghis Khan after having been acclaimed as Khaqan, as overlord of the federation, by the assembly of princes and chieftains, the Khuriltai, in 1206. Right up to the time of his death he led them in conquering large areas of what is now Russian Turkestan, driving the Jurchen-Chin south of the Huangho and completely wiping the Tangut Hsi-Hsia state off the map. He already had Chinese, or sinized Jurchen, in his service, who not only showed the Mongols how to lay siege to Chinese towns, but also how to administer an agrarian and urban society like China's. Even so, the conquest of China took over half a century. The Jurchen state gave way under the Mongol onslaughts in 1234, but only in 1279 did the third Great Khan, Kublai (reigned 1260–94), break down the last pocket of Sung resistance in the far south, near Canton. That was eight years after he had proclaimed the new Yüan dynasty. For the first time the whole of China lay under a foreign conqueror. The subjection of the densely populated, extensive agrarian realm to a relatively small tribal society of nomadic origin led to a total restructuring of Chinese society. The traditional educated elite, especially in the last areas to remain under the rule of the Southern Sung, were excluded from government. For the first time, they sank to the level of the governed, together with the landed elite, who were at least allowed to keep most of their possessions; they became mere taxpayers, and moreover bore most of the burden of taxation, since the north had largely been given to the Mongol aristocracy as bounty. Such sudden restratification, affecting every inhabitant of the empire, must be regarded as unique. At best it is comparable with the far simpler restructuring of the early Chou period. In view of the substantially more complex fabric of Chinese society under the Sung, and its greater distinctions, consolidated by the custom of centuries, what the Mongols tried to do must be regarded as anachronistic.

The population of the Mongol empire comprised four groups, with gradations of rights. The race of foreign rulers was dominant. The second rank was accorded to the 'people with coloured eyes' (se-mu-jen): aliens living and working in the empire, who belonged to neither the Chinese nor Mongol races, nor to the Jurchen, but were principally of central Asian or Middle Eastern origins; Persians, Syrians, Turks, Tanguts etc. The inhabitants of north China (Han-jen: 'people of Han') came third. These were Chinese, or more or less sinized Kitan or Jurchen, who had lived in the Liao and Chin states for centuries. The largest section of the population, the inhabitants of the former Southern Sung state, had the fewest political rights. They were officially called simply 'people of the south' (Nan-jen). Unofficially, however, they were often described as 'southern barbarians' (man-tzu). This division gravely affected the previously privileged southern Chinese upper classes. Furthermore they must have felt profoundly insulted to hear themselves called 'barbarians' in their own language by, of all people, the 'uncivilized' nomadic Mongols. Although the Mongol state remained throughout a military dictatorship, the conquerors could not avoid building up an administrative substructure. They adopted formal institutions from the T'ang, Sung and Chin administrations, but considerably altered the way they functioned. At the tip of the pyramid were, as before, three offices: the Central Chancellory (chung-shu-sheng) in charge of civil affairs, the Privy State Council (shu-mi-yüan) in charge of military affairs, and the Censorate (*yü-shih-t'ai*) to supervise the entire administration. The Six Ministries (*liu-pu*) were retained without any important changes. The separate regions of the Mongol empire were governed directly by officials of the Central Chancellory, as had been the Chin practice. The 'provinces' (*sheng*) were thus to begin with 'branch offices of the Central Chancellory' (*hsing chung-shu-sheng*). This proved an important measure in establishing absolutism in China. But like the other conquerors and indeed the Chinese emperors, the Mongols found the immense host of Chinese professional civil servants indispensable to the government of the immense empire. The old type of state examinations ceased, however; all the reliable officials in the north, who were capable of running the selection process, had more pressing duties to fulfil. The numerous qualified educated people in the south were sorely needed, but met the conquerors with a solid front of non-cooperation. To the Chinese of the south, and more especially to the educated ones among them, the Mongols were and remained savages, uncivilized barbarians. Faced with this tacit rather than open hostility, but also to maintain the distance between conquerors and conquered, the Mongols employed numerous aliens, particularly 'Tartars, Saracens and Christians', as Marco Polo recounted, which did not exactly help to endear them to their subjects. According to later Chinese historians, the Mongols never won respect or acceptance from the majority of the population of the empire. They temporarily occupied the empire, but never legitimized their rule morally. Unfortunately this construction did nothing to alter the facts of the matter.

Not only the administrative dilemma threatened the Mongols. Economic difficulties existed which eventually undermined their position more effectively than political factors. There were two problems in particular. Firstly the Mongols had made paper money the only legal tender. All coins were withdrawn from circulation, allegedly to make Lamaist devotional objects; but there was possibly a connection between this and the ban on weapons enforced for the Chinese. Like the late Sung rulers, the Mongols circulated paper money without backing. Consequently foreign trade and the taxation system finally collapsed. Difficulties also arose in supplying the capital city Ta-tu (Peking) with grain; periodically it ran out altogether, through a combination of marauders, sabotage and corruption. Finally, an open struggle for power broke out among the various Mongol princes and lords. This engaged their forces and at times took on a truly

100

'barbarian' aspect. From about 1330 a never-ending series of uprisings confronted the foreign rulers and before long they lacked any effective countermeasures. For once, rarely in Chinese history, the government fell directly due to radical division between the rulers and the ruled. Probably this was because the normal antagonisms were aggravated by racial and cultural divisions. This special combination of circumstances has frequently been interpreted by modern historians as the beginning of Chinese nationalism. It is an open question, whether genuine integration of the personal and institutional potential of China could have averted the threat to the foreign central government. The experiences of both Mongols and Chinese were at all events absorbed by Chinese history; another race of conquerors, the Manchu, were to take them to heart a few centuries later.

The ultimate victor to emerge from the swarm of rebels was Chu Yüan-chang (1328–98), a man of humble origins, like Liu Pang, the founder of the Han dynasty. Chu had spent some time in a Buddhist monastery which, like many others at that date and probably not least because of the preference shown to Lamaism by the Mongols, had become a kind of spiritual centre of the opposition to the foreign yoke. Chu Yüan-chang was soon the leader of a ruthless and efficient fighting force, with which he eliminated his rivals and increasingly forced the Mongols to retreat. The first city of any size that fell to him was Nanking, in 1356. Not only the impoverished sections of the population supported him. Among the traditional educated elite and the large landowners he found an ever readier following, in proportion as his campaign assumed an anti-Mongol, quasi-nationalist character, and lost sight of its socio-revolutionary origins. Even before his conquest of the north and the capital Ta-tu (Peking) in 1368, Chu Yüan-chang had set up an efficient local administration in the Yangtse region, and thereby created one of the most important preconditions of sovereignty. With this nuclear state as his foothold, he eventually conquered the whole empire. After the fall of Ta-tu he had the Ming dynasty proclaimed in Nanking. This was the first occasion on which the empire was so conquered and united from the south, a fact reflecting the gradual shift in the empire's centre of gravity, during the previous five hundred years, from the north-west and the central Huangho region to the south-east and the lower Yangtse. The transfer of power had taken place relatively quickly: there had not been time for the establishment of intermediate dynasties worthy of the name, as there were between the T'ang and the Sung. How deeply the idea of the empire's unity, and its possible division, had become ingrained in the historical consciousness of the Chinese is illustrated by the first sentence of the *Romance of the Three Kingdoms* (*San-kuo yen-i*) written at the end of the Yüan regime and the beginning of the Ming: 'If the empire [*t'ien-hsia*] has been divided for long, it will certainly be united, if it has been united for long, it will certainly be divided'.

As will by now be clear, to consolidate its power a new dynasty had to take over administration of the whole empire with all speed. In most cases the founding emperor started by taking over the institutions left by earlier dynasties and developed new forms at his leisure. It is astonishing how much of the administrative experience of past generations retained its vitality for centuries. It is a phenomenon that throws light on the characterization of the history of traditional China as 'change within tradition' (Kracke). Consequently, administration under the Ming emperors was first and foremost, just as in earlier eras, an instrument of power, and not a system intended to serve the people to whom it was applied. Any benefit they derived from it was and remained incidental to the object of the 'administration of the world' (*ching-shih*), which was nothing other than the continuing security of the central government.

Initially the Ming administration did not differ essentially from that of the Sung or, to a certain extent, the Yüan. But Chu Yüan-chang, who was canonized as Emperor T'ai-tsu from 1368 to 1398, never overcame completely his distrust of the educated classes whose antecedents were so different from his own. Following a purge, the principal victims of which were his chancellor Hu Wei-yung (d. 1380) and other senior civil servants, he ordained changes at the topmost level of the administration that rendered the emperor's own position even more absolute than it had already been since the Sung. The organs of government that had mediated between the emperor and the executive, especially the Secretariat-Chancellory, were dissolved; the office of chancellor was abolished; the emperor became not merely the highest authority, but the chief administrator as well. T'ai-tsu thus erected institutions whose foundations had been laid by the Sung emperors. This and comparable steps have earned him epithets like autocrat, despot and occasionally even totalitarian ruler. But the emperors of China had been autocrats before his reign, and not a few had been despots too. To call him a totalitarian ruler is really anachronistic, in view of the considerable hindrances to communication that still existed. But undoubtedly it was under T'ai-tsu that Chinese absolutism, fed by Chinese and alien tributaries, launched on its classic course, took on the form that European travellers commented on, approvingly or disapprovingly, from the sixteenth century onwards. A single example, from court ceremonial, illustrates the growth of absolutism over the centuries and its culmination under the Ming. The T'ang emperors permitted high officials to be seated in their presence; the Sung emperors required them to remain standing; the Ming emperors and later the Manchu-Ch'ing adopted the Mongol custom that required even the very highest of officials to prostrate himself on the floor throughout an audience. Even those who worked most closely with the emperor, in the day-to-day administration of affairs, were obliged to obey this regulation. Following the abolition of the chancellorship, these duties fell to 'Grand Secretaries' (*ta-hsüeh-shih*), most of whom were graduates of the imperial Han-lin academy and later formed an informal 'Inner Cabinet' (*nei-ko*). The Grand Secretaries advised the emperor, but also had ceremonial and bureaucratic duties, notably the preparation of all written communications. They were not allowed to act independently. Other aids to the imperial administration included the Chief Military Command (*wu-chün tu-tu fu*) and the Supervisory Censorate (*tu-ch'a yüan*). This threefold system was mirrored at the level of the 'provinces' (*sheng*), now the highest branch of the regional administration. The government of each province consisted of three authorities (*san-ssu*) which were directly connected with their equivalents in the capital: the Civil Authority (*ch'eng-hsüan pu-cheng ssu*), the Military Authority (*tu-chih-hui ssu*) and the Legal Authority (*t'i-hsing an-ch'a ssu*). Local administrations mostly remained undivided. There were now, however, three kinds of local unit: 'prefecture' (*fu*), 'sub-prefecture' (*chou*) and 'district' (*hsien*). During the Ming period regional administrative powers, too, were agglomerated, at first on a temporary basis, then permanently to an increasing extent from the sixteenth century onwards, and placed in the hands of 'Grand Coordinators' or 'Governors' (*hsün-fu*). On principle, local officials, and regional officials, too, to a certain extent, were not allowed to serve in their home province. Naturally this system benefited the centre completely only when a strong personality occupied the throne. The next emperor but one after T'ai-tsu was one such. The first Ming emperor was succeeded by a grandson (reigned 1399–1403), who was forcibly deposed after a few years by his uncle, T'ai-tsu's fourth son, supported by troops who owed their allegiance to him personally. Usurper though he was, the third Ming emperor, whose dynastic title was Ch'eng-tsu (reigned 1403–25), was an able administrator. Chinese historians have never completely agreed about him. In 1421 Ch'eng-tsu moved the capital to Peking. Apparently this was mainly because his personal domains were in that area. But it also accorded with an overriding principle of the position of the political centre of gravity in Chinese history: China's capital was always also, in a certain sense, the principal city of central Asia. Ch'eng-tsu surpassed his father's absolute sovereignty in employing personal assistants who were to a certain extent extra-constitutional. As so often in the more remote past these assistants were eunuchs, whose employment in the civil service had been expressly forbidden by T'ai-tsu. The inspection of provincial affairs, direction of military enterprises and diplomatic missions were now entrusted to eunuchs. Henceforth disputes between the eunuchs and the regular civil service featured regularly throughout almost all of the Ming era. When eunuchs were in the ascendancy at court, their government was pilloried by the chroniclers and historiographers, who were all of course members of the civil service. Although their viewpoint, as well as that of eye-witnesses, is not free of personal bias and emotions, it appears that the eunuchs were exceptionally opportunist and ruthless in their dealings. Wei Chung-hsien (1568–1627) was a typical example. Wei started his career in the service of the Empress Mother. When the degenerate Hsi-tsung (reigned 1621–27), a fifteen-year-old with no knowledge of affairs, ascended the throne, he appointed Wei, who was a close friend of his nurse, to direct the government on his behalf. Aided by a small group of other eunuchs and self-seeking opportunists from the ranks of the civil service, Wei instituted a regime based on terrorization and the use of informers and which was directed equally against all ranks of society. The utmost in taxes and tribute was extorted from the people; critics of Wei at the court and in the provinces were removed from office; the defence of the northern frontier, already under severe pressure from the Manchu, was further weakened by the dismissal of commanders who did not meet with Wei's approval. The only section of society who could have prevented Wei's abuses of power was the civil service and educated elite. They were, however, divided and at first unable to offer united resistance. Several factions, the best known that associated with the Tung-lin academy in Wu-hsi (Kiangsu), contended for influence. They disabled themselves in abstract arguments about

104

political, moral and philosophical principles; the integration of absolutism into the structure of Confucian thought was one of the main topics. Not until physical extermination threatened the Tunglin group did practical opposition materialize (1626). It had little effect on Wei Chung-hsien's influence. Only the accession of a new emperor in 1627, who appointed his own political favourites to positions of power, brought Wei's rule to an end. Wei's career demonstrates to what great extent government and the executive still depended on personal factors. It also illustrates, however, that although the civil service and educated elite regarded themselves in the Ming period as the guarantors of justice and order, they were permanently at odds with themselves, that is, with the central power, according to how they viewed their obligations to the common good on the one hand and to their own interests on the other. Only when they had a part to play in the government was the conflict apparently reconciled. For this reason the educated elite only balanced the central ruler's absolute power in so far as they were themselves excluded from power and were threatened with the loss of their well-paid posts. In spite of various attempts this threat was in any case never carried out with complete success. In the early years of the Ming regime much thought was given to strengthening the state economy. Numerous measures were introduced, such as redistribution of land ownership, reclamation of fallow land, foundation of labour colonies for the poorest of the rural population and for vagrants, an almost egalitarian tax register and much else that might have achieved that end. But by the late fifteenth century the system of taxation and statute labour had become entangled in a chaotic web that harmed the state and was more than the people could bear. The 'Unitary System' (*i-t'iao-pien fa*), commonly known as the 'single whip system', was supposed to furnish a remedy. It was based on a fundamentally reasonable principle, namely to re-organize all taxes and duties into a small number of categories and to collect equivalent amounts in silver. But its implementation was slow and haphazard, varying from one place to the next; and the scheme remained a torso.

In the long run, the ruinous financial situation, the fluctuating grasp on power at the top, the demoralized civil service, led also to a loss of authority in the provinces. This in turn undermined the stability of the central government. When famine broke out in the 1630s in north China, the organs of government were unable to prevent anti-dynastic cells forming, which eventually overthrew the rule of the Ming

105

emperors. Two men distinguished themselves in particular, Li Tzu-ch'eng (c. 1605–45) and Chang Hsien-chung (c. 1605–47), both of whom are best described as professional bandit chiefs. At first both operated in north China, where they managed to form effective fighting forces from the oppressed and discontented rural population. Some members of the educated class joined them too. With their troops behind them, and with the aid of their educated adherents, both founded their own states, one after the other, complete with administrative machinery, their own coinage and a centralized military organization. Li Tzu-ch'eng established himself initially in Hupei, Honan and Shensi (1643); Chang Hsien-chung had control from 1644 of the greater part of Ssechuan. But the disintegration of the empire apparently denoted by this situation proved only a short interlude. Neither of the two chieftains managed to maintain his rule, although Li Tzu-ch'eng succeeded in taking Peking in 1644 and drove the last Ming emperor to suicide. The loss of order and the power vacuum in China profited a foreign race, the Manchu.

Like the Mongols at the time of Jenghis Khan, the Manchu had achieved unity at a moment when there was a marked drop in the power of the dynasty ruling China to resist them. The Manchu were a branch of the Jurchen, who had already ruled the northern half of China once, under the name of Chin. Without the risk of being sinized by actually ruling a Chinese population, the members of the new alliance learned from China how to organize a state. Nurhachi (1559–1626), who unified the most important of the Jurchen tribes under his rule, by peaceful means or by force, in the course of three decades, gained practical experience in governing a Chinese agrarian population when, in 1618, he seized the larger part of the Liaotung peninsula, which belonged to the Ming empire. With the help of Chinese advisers who either were refugees or had been taken prisoner, Nurhachi and his successor Abahai (1592–1643) gradually built up a state on the Chinese pattern. They founded a stable military organization, the so-called Banners (ch'i), which on the one hand took into account the tribal character of the alliance, called Manchu from 1635 onwards, and on the other effectively protected the leaders from danger. Thus years before the Manchu overran China, two administrative organs already existed which favoured the centralization of power and were prerequisites for assuming power in China. The Manchu leaders also systematically promoted Confucianization, the political and ideological alignment of their society. While rebels were struggling to seize power in the Ming empire in the 1630s, on the far side of its northern frontier a state was already in formation that possessed distinct Chinese characteristics in organization and aspirations. Abahai made his first thrust deep into northern China in 1636, and although repulsed by the Ming, he founded the Ch'ing dynasty in the same year in Mukden, thereby making a formal claim to the Chinese throne.

When Li Tzu-ch'eng attacked Peking in 1644 the emperor sent for his general Wu San-kuei (1612–78), who was stationed in Liaotung. The city fell before Wu got there, and as he retreated before Li Tzu-ch'eng, he called on the Manchu for help, who were already waiting on the frontier. Together they defeated Li. Once in China, the Manchu pressed on southwards and, with the support of Wu San-kuei and other Chinese generals, they conquered the entire Ming empire within the space of twenty years. In 1673 three of the most famous Chinese generals, including Wu, rose against the Manchu and proclaimed their own dynasties in the south. It was nearly another decade before the Manchu brought the whole realm under their control. Their success was only partly due to military superiority. A not inconsiderable factor in the establishment of the new regime was the support of the wealthy and educated upper class, whom the new rulers had courted from the very start. Over the centuries this class had developed a dual relationship with succeeding dynasties, nurtured in the last analysis by a single motive, the preservation of its own position. The upper class was at once the prop and the corrective to central absolutism. Its promotion of its own interests could undermine a dynasty or, when it came to a change of power, could alone make it possible. A new dynasty, particularly a foreign one, had to be sure of the support of the landowning, educated upper class, who could guarantee stability on the periphery of the empire, i.e. in the outlying provinces. In these circumstances, it was usually not so much their political privileges that concerned the wealthy Chinese as their economic advantages, and these were left inviolate by the Ch'ing, once they had requisitioned enough land for their Banner troops. More: an important difference between the Ch'ing and the Mongol rulers three centuries earlier was that the class of large landowners and civil servants maintained its status of a distinct, superior social class. In this way, with a few exceptions who were not prepared to cooperate with the foreign 'barbarians', those Chinese who possessed wealth and education became the most important internal allies of the Manchu emperors.

As a foreign dynasty the Manchu, like the Mongols and other invaders, were faced with the double necessity, not only of taking a firm hold on the administration of the empire, but also of preserving their own ethnic identity. So far as the latter was concerned, strict regulations were laid down forbidding even the common Manchu any kind of fraternization with the Chinese, or imitation of Chinese ways. At the same time, however, the Manchu emperors took serious and successful steps to promote education in Confucianism. This on the one hand, was a way of commanding the respect and recognition of the Chinese educated class. But, on the other, it proved over several generations at least as effective a means of sinizing the Manchurian upper class as intermarriage would have been. The Manchu adopted the administrative machinery of the Ming with only a few alterations, but they made one striking innovation in the actual staffing of the organization. Nearly all the senior posts, both at the centre and in the provinces, were duplicated and held by one Chinese and one non-Chinese official, usually a Manchu, but sometimes also a Mongol. In this way they took advantage of the administrative experience of the Chinese officials and checked anti-Manchurianism in those circles. Simultaneously they prevented their own men from accumulating too much power and establishing a bureaucracy. Both officials were equal in rank and equally responsible. In regional administration the Manchu institutionalized the offices of 'governor' (hsün-fu) and 'governor general' (tsung-tu). These had been introduced under the Ming, but not filled as a matter of regular practice. The governor general, always a Manchu in the early years, headed the administration of two or more provinces. European literature of the time always called him the 'Viceroy'. The third of the Manchu emperors to live in China, Shih-tsung (reigned 1723–36, known as the Yung-cheng Emperor from the title given to his reign), who apparently acquired the crown by stratagem, strengthened the central power further. He created a new, informal, advisory body, the Council of State (chün-chi ch'u) (1729), to replace the Inner Cabinet. This organization had been taken over from the Ming by the Manchu, but had meanwhile become over-independent and somewhat ponderous in its operations. At first the new council concerned itself mainly with military planning. But it soon developed responsibilities in every direction, and briefed the emperor on all his decisions. That meant, in effect, virtually every governmental decision of importance; even the instructions issued by the central civil administration, the Six Ministries (liu-pu), to the provincial authorities had to be authorized by the emperor, unless they dealt with matters of the purest routine.

Shih-tsung's economic and financial measures were also decisive in stabilizing his rule. He introduced a less complicated unit tax, to be paid in money or goods according to choice; he tried by strict regulations and controls to limit the excessively high tax demands made by officials. To prevent them making arbitrary supplementary demands on the taxpayers, he raised their salaries and pegged the amounts of supplement permitted. All the same, there were practically no controls on the size of land holdings, so that the accumulation of estates went on unhindered. And as always, it was easier for the large landowners to keep their taxes within moderate bounds. This meant that in practice the burden of taxation was regressive. Significantly, too, after Shih-tsung's death the elite of the civil service, who were essential to the Manchu emperors, could once again levy taxes as they wished. Before the eighteenth century had run its course, both factors had led to renewed abuses by the upper classes of their privileges and intolerable burdening of the mass of the population.

The Manchu emperors displayed remarkable efficiency and acumen in forestalling almost all the dangers, which in one combination or another had plagued and finally overthrown previous dynasties. Relatives of the imperial wives and eunuchs were barred from high office; the imperial princes were not allowed to command Banners; almost every military unit, including those on the frontiers, were under mixed Chinese–Manchurian command; external military threats were checked by political measures and extensive campaigning; the educated and wealthy Chinese elite were firmly integrated in the dynastic state by a complex system of controls and privileges. There was no way, however, of preventing favourites from seizing and enjoying power, if an emperor chose or was compelled to withdraw from the multifarious burdens of government. The prime example cited by Chinese historians is the career of Ho-shen, a Manchurian Banner officer (1750–99). Under his aegis corruption rose to almost astronomical proportions at every level of the administration and in every department of the state, including the army. Ho-shen's meteoric rise from an officer in the imperial bodyguard to the highest positions in the state is attributed to the senility of Emperor Kao-tsung (reigned 1736–96, known as the Ch'ien-lung Emperor). Kao-tsung had been brilliant in his youth, but from the mid-1770s, as he grew older, his liking for the young, intelligent Ho-shen steadily increased, and he

109

trusted him blindly. Ho-shen knew how to make the best of his good fortune and he was supreme in the empire for over twenty years, until the death of his imperial protector. Under him the Banners received only minimum training and equipment and lost their efficiency. Likewise the civil service degenerated under his direction into a corrupt but also harassed and intimidated *apparat*.

Neither the civil nor the military organization proved adequate to tackle the problems that arose in the nineteenth century. This failure is not attributable, however, to Ho-shen alone. Never before in Chinese history had the ruling dynasty and the upper class that served it been confronted with problems of such a magnitude. Their failure within traditional norms and practices merely underlines their impotence before current developments. The population explosion under way since the eighteenth century was unique in Chinese history. The administrative machinery had not expanded, nor had adequate economic measures been taken, to cope with it. The result was a progressive deterioration in the provisions for large sections of the population and the growth of an administrative vacuum in large areas of the country. Nor had China ever before been confronted with the superior technology, ideological certainties and political determination of the West, whose aggression she was increasingly powerless to resist, intellectually or materially. After the defeats of the Opium War (1839–42) the Ch'ing were forced to surrender their sovereignty bit by bit. And as the authority of the dynastic centre crumbled, so too did China's identity as a state.

Compared with the tensions between rulers and subjects, and between China and the rest of the world, the tension between the centre and the periphery was of little significance in the nineteenth century. The growth of peripheral power, particularly marked in the second half of the century, originated in mass unrest and the encroachment of external enemies. To meet these threats a large proportion of the civil and the military authorities were moved from the capital to the provinces. Chinese officials, above all, grew in influence and power, as the centre declined. But it is significant that governors and generals such as Tseng Kuo-fan (1811–72), Li Hung-chang (1823–1901) and Yüan Shih-k'ai (1859–1916) identified themselves with the ruling Confucian dynasty: although it was foreign it embodied the traditional values of the Chinese upper class, in the face of lower-class rebels and foreign invaders. Only when the decay in the central power's efficiency was well advanced, following a series of defeats by foreign enemies (e.g. the Sino-Japanese War 1894–95, the Boxer Intervention 1900–1901) and after some half-hearted attempts at reform (including abolition of the traditional examination system in 1905), that the peripheral forces seriously contributed to the isolation of the dynasty. Only then was the gulf between the Chinese and the Manchu articulated among the upper classes too. When rebels invoking the name of Sun Yat-sen finally rose openly against the regime in 1911, in the central Chinese town of Wuchang (Wuhan), the now merely nominal rule of the Manchu collapsed within months. Before the end of the year all the provincial governors, except those of the three northern provinces, had repudiated the central government. The dynasty formally abdicated on 12 February 1912; it was the end of more than two thousand years of imperial rule in China. But it ended less through centrifugal tendencies than through the traditional system's total unsuitability to a changed world.

China's exceptionally long history is better suited than that of any other historical continuum lasting into the twentieth century to illustrate long-term developments and tendencies. Such a process of abstraction risks, however, a resulting historical relief too shallow to be of more than minimal value. With this drawback in mind, here follows a schematic summary of the development of political power in the heartland of traditional China.

The specifically Chinese pattern of power at the centre and power at the periphery was at no point laid down once and for all – under the Chou for instance. There were quantifiable changes, even if over very long periods. There is no mistaking the general trend towards absolutism and creation of structural and ideological uniformity in the social fabric of the subject population. But the trend did undergo interruptions. The periods, first longer, then shorter, when the empire was divided resulted from power building up on the periphery, and of centrifugal tendencies, especially in earlier Chinese history. During later centuries, roughly from the Sung dynasty onwards, tendencies more typically fluctuated within the framework of the dynastic configurations. Meanwhile the overall shape of China had by then become virtually indestructible. Characteristic of a dynasty's life-cycle were the pre-eminence, initially, of several strong, dynamic emperors, and subsequently of the upper classes, especially of the higher civil servants who belonged to them. In the first, growth, phase, decisive steps were taken to stabilize power and reinforce the central authority. In the second, bureaucratic, phase, the government was to all intents

111

and purposes an oligarchy. This always tended to maintain the *status quo*, especially with regard to the possession and influence of the governing class itself.

THE RULERS AND THE RULED

The first part of this chapter concentrated on the tension between power at the centre and power on the periphery. But that was only one influence on the shaping of Chinese history. Another was the tension between the governing classes, whether in power at the centre or on the periphery, and the mass of the population. Just as polarity between centre and periphery was centrifugal and particularist, so tension between rulers and ruled was articulated by continual popular uprisings. Mao Tse-tung has said only these were truly propellant forces in Chinese history, since each one dealt the feudal order a blow and thus 'to a greater or lesser degree advanced the development of the productive forces in society'. This view is debatable. Not infrequently popular rebellions did produce changes, usually of the individuals in power. But they hardly transformed the social structure, even though some Chinese Marxist historians believe they gave the farming population greater influence on the means of production and the society of their time (Ch'i Li-huang). It is fair comment to say that in the past the Chinese were by far the most rebellious of all civilized races, but at the same time the least revolutionary (Meadows).

From a very early date the organization and the control of the masses were a central concern of the dominant elements in Chinese society, in their own interests. Bauer's interpretation of the specific form the controls took as nothing more than a 'simple function of the gigantic dimensions of time, space and population' is not easy to accept. According to tradition, Shang Yang, the chief minister in the Ch'in kingdom from 361 to 338 BC, introduced a system of mutual supervision and answerability. Under this the general population, until then most likely standing in some loose clan relationship with the landlords or feudal lords, was for the first time brought under the control of a largely anonymous government. Such a system could only work effectively within close-knit neighbourhood communities and although no express reference is made to families as such, one may assume that the members of each community were mostly interrelated. At all events, throughout the imperial era the family, the unit in which the individual was absorbed and held in check, was

112

generally an integral part of the system. The principle was perpetuated of families and neighbourhoods being responsible for each of their members. Once again the significance of the family, even among the lower classes, is thus underlined, as an essential element of the Chinese state. Possibly the family was the most important 'organ' of the state in that area of it that lay beyond the immediate reach of the administration. The Confucians' persistent idealization of the family hierarchy stands revealed in this light as an ideology of the ruling class. Most significant of all, the social class that regarded itself as Confucian first and foremost, and made that one of the major justifications of its right to govern, did not hesitate to adopt Legalist principles, such as the system of mutual control and answerability, when it was a matter of stabilizing the social position of the lower classes and ensuring their absolute obedience.

But these small units at the base of Chinese society were answerable for more than the political good behaviour of their members. The system was repeatedly re-organized and given new or different responsibilities. Under the Northern Wei Emperor Hsiao-wen (reigned 471–99) every five families were joined up to make a neighbourhood (*lin*), every five neighbourhoods a village (*li*) and every five villages a local alliance (*tang*), and made wholly responsible for collecting their own taxes. In the Sung period the reformer Wang An-shih (1021–86) grouped every ten families in a collective responsibility group (*pao*) which had to raise its own militia, with which to provide its own defence and maintain its own peace and public order. Still under the Sung, Chu Hsi instigated the organization of every ten families into a 'decade' (*chia*), one of whose duties was to guarantee every member's contribution to the public granaries. There were two systems of organization under the Ming emperors, the smallest unit of which was again the family. The two systems existed side by side, but did not coincide exactly. A 'village decade' (*li-chia*) consisted of 110 families, and the headship (*chang*) passed in rotation among the ten richest families in it. This organization was responsible for providing labour forces and collecting taxes. A 'community decade' (*pao-chia*), which consisted in theory of one hundred families, was a self-policing organization responsible for political good behaviour. Under the Ch'ing the two systems largely merged and grew considerably – possibly a reflection of increasing population density. Theoretically ten families made a 'register' (*p'ai*), a hundred families a 'decade' (*chia*) and a thousand families a 'community' (*pao*). The headman (*chang*) was elected by the member families; none the less the system was in no way autonomous. The form of the organization and its purposes, which included the surveillance of public morality, registration of the population, the supervision of crafts and trades, policing and much else besides, were controlled by the authorities through the local landowners, to whose ranks the headmen usually belonged. Not content with the power accrued to them through recruitment from their families to the civil service, the landowning upper classes found this another convenient means of running local affairs, from the Ming period, if not earlier. It gave them opportunities to avoid paying taxes, over and above the allowances that legally went with holding office, by such means as falsifying entries in the registers. Naturally it was the weaker members of the community who had to make up for their evasions. It was throughout the wealthy and well-educated – the upper classes – who profited most from these systems, which were devised to uphold and strengthen whoever happened to hold the central power.

This system of organization was of course most efficient in agricultural districts, where the population was unlikely to fluctuate or move away. In the towns it could only be brought to bear on permanent residents like shopkeepers and artisans. It was extremely difficult, on the other hand, to exercise any control by this means over mobile groups of the population, such as miners who went wherever there was work for them, itinerant salesmen, sailors or fishermen. So far as possible such people were included in the system by their relatives being made responsible for them, however far away they might live. The system also only worked when the state, through its agents, was willing and able to carry out the threatened reprisals. Necessarily these reprisals fell also on the heads of those members of the upper classes who usually represented the state. If the state was unable to act, or if its measures were intolerably oppressive, then the unit set up to protect the interests of the government was very easily converted into an independent association, protecting itself and its own interests, and thus the nucleus of an insurrection. The familial system and the neighbourhood organization founded on it remained a source of political subordination until the twentieth century. But potentially it equally endangered the state. Sun Yat-sen (1866–1924) had good reason to regret the widespread clannishness of family and local interests, which he berated as an 'excess of freedom' and condemned as a hindrance to national unity.

114

The postulate of the Confucian philosopher Meng-tzu (371–289 BC), that a ruler was legitimized by the quiescent acceptance from the subject population, has already been mentioned. The reverse side of this formula was interpreted as a 'right of rebellion', to which insurgents of later periods often appealed. It is true that the principle allowed only one justification of an uprising, namely success. Unsuccessful rebels were condemned without mercy, by historians as well.

According to tradition, the first 'plebeian' (Teng Ssu-yü) insurrection in China was set in motion in 209 BC by a poor agricultural labourer called Ch'en She (d. 208 BC). It is hard to make out whether it really was the first of its kind. There had been uprisings and disturbances before; what was new about the movement was that it was directed against a central ruler and his organs of government. The originality or otherwise of the movement is less interesting than that it already bore characteristics typical of the majority of later risings. These were, namely, the protagonists' tendency to join forces with the ruling class, or the former ruling class, and the aimlessness of their organization and programme. Marxist commentators in particular have condemned this as a severe weakness, calling it 'vagabondism' (*liu-k'ou chu-i*). Hardly had Ch'en She acquired a handful of followers than he called himself 'King of Ch'u'. He was incapable of creating a disciplined body from the former forced labourers and slaves who followed him; and he had no clear political concepts, nor even a revolutionary programme. Ch'en She was not the only one to rise after the death of the first Ch'in emperor. New 'kings' sprang up all over the empire, with larger or smaller numbers of followers, to fight against the government forces sent out to oppose them, and against each other. Finally there emerged victorious from the fighting another rebel leader of non-aristocratic origins: Liu Pang (d. 195 BC), the founder of the Han dynasty. Liu Pang began public life as a 'village officer' (*t'ing-chang*) in the service of the state, but then used his position to gain followers, who became 'bandits' when he revolted against his superiors. He later allied himself to the great aristocratic opponent of the Ch'in, Hsiang Yü (d. 206 BC), but soon outmanoeuvered him.

The Ch'in destruction of the feudal order of the Chou period prompted the aristocracy to refuse allegiance to the new dynasty. The Ch'in also had difficulty in winning over the mass of the population, who blamed them for burdens unknown before, or which were

115

at least extended. Consequently, unrest was greatest in those areas which had come under Ch'in suzerainty most recently. One refuge from the growing load, which was often apparent slavery, as the population were simply conscripted to build roads, canals, defences and palaces, was the anonymity of banditry. Bands of such fugitives had to steal their food, usually from the state granaries or from large landowners. Merely taking enough to keep body and soul together grew all too easily into wholesale plundering. Thus the bandits became part of a tradition already introduced in the Time of the Warring States with the so-called 'Knights Errant' (*yu-hsieh*). The Knights Errant had earned the reputation of drawing their swords in strictly circumscribed cases in order to win 'victory for the cause of justice' (*ch'i-i*; the modern Chinese expression for 'revolt'). In practice this usually meant protecting individuals, sometimes the destitute, against the abuses of those in positions of power. The mixture of fear and sympathy that the Knights aroused continued to be extended by the general population towards the bandits who succeeded them. The Knights usually rode alone, but the first alliances for mutual protection and for safeguarding shared beliefs were apparently already forming within the Time of the Warring States. These were the forerunners of the secret societies which played so important a part in the history of rebellion in China (Franke/Trauzettel). Rigidly organized societies or sects feature particularly in the anti-Confucian, relatively egalitarian tradition of the Mohists.

But the formation of groups of bandits and insurgent societies resulted not only from tyrannous extremism on the part of the rulers, but also from their decline. This was particularly so at times when this led to local disruption of the economy and created an administrative vacuum. Not infrequently this development coincided with devastating natural catastrophes. Traditional commentators always placed a moral interpretation on such coincidences. Although the natural catastrophes were not themselves provoked by a ruler's weakness, the severity of their effects was exactly proportioned to his incapacity or cynicism. Thus, if not averted in time, they could hasten the end of the *status quo*. Similarly, increased insurgency and banditry could also be interpreted as a sign of a dynasty's approaching end.

A situation of this kind arose at the end of the first century BC. Various forms of unrest existed from 22 BC onwards, which allowed Wang Mang (45 BC to AD 23) to usurp the throne of the ruling Han dynasty and found his own. His radical programme of reforms, however, succeeded in alienating not only the rich landowners but also large sections of the ordinary rural population. When the Huangho burst its dikes in the year 11, causing great hardship and distress in the neighbourhood of the capital, large numbers of the population began to flock southwards. In the region that is now the province of Shantung, which was especially badly hit, the farmers who had lost their land banded together and rose in open rebellion against the government in the year 18. There are indications that the nucleus of the movement was a Taoist-inspired secret society, although this is disputed. The leaders certainly do not appear to have been members of the very lowest, most poverty-stricken class of society. Instead like many later insurgent leaders, they seem to have been tradesmen, moderately wealthy landowners, and even to have included the occasional local official. In order to distinguish themselves from the troops of Wang Mang, and perhaps also as a sign of magic affiliation, the rebels dyed their eyebrows red. The choice of red was not without significance: it was the colour of the 'legitimate' Han dynasty. Red was the colour chosen by rebels on several later occasions, notably towards the end of the Yüan period and under the Ch'ing emperors. In both these cases the dynasties in power were not Han Chinese, but foreigners. The revolt of the 'Red Eyebrows' (Ch'ih-mei) quickly spread. Apparently in order to legitimize their action they conferred the title of emperor on a scion of the house of Han. When, after overthrowing Wang Mang with the help of the Red Eyebrows in 23, their nominee tried to double-cross them and evade giving their leaders fiefs, they turned against him. But no strong man emerged from their own ranks to claim the throne, nor did they manage to establish an effective administration in any of the areas they overran. In the year 27 they surrendered to the first of the Later Han emperors, who had greatly profited by both the preceding struggle and the Red Eyebrows' incompetence.

The insurgent movements which formed towards the end of the Later Han dynasty were the first whose origins and intellectual foundations undoubtedly lay in religious sects. These sects, the 'Way of Five Bushels of Rice' (Wu-tou-mi-tao), based in what is now Ssechuan, and the 'Great Way of Peace' (T'ai-p'ing-tao) on the Shantung peninsula, were born of the popular Taoism that had grown up during the Han era. Their leaders practised faith healing and celebrated public ceremonies of casting out sin, which allegedly involved human sacrifice and orgiastic rites. They had spent much time as itinerant preachers and had thus gathered large followings. When both these sects rose in open revolt, independently of each other, in 184, they took the administration, the eunuchs and civil servants who had been at loggerheads for several years, completely by surprise. Since the adherents of the northern sect wore yellow scarves on their heads, the movement became known as the 'Yellow Turbans' (*Huang-chin*). The turbans were not merely for identification but also had a symbolic meaning. Yellow was the colour of the chief deity of Popular Taoism, the 'Yellow Emperor' (*huang-ti*). At the same time it also referred to 'earth', the 'element' (*hsing*) which, according to contemporary cosmological beliefs, was due to triumph over the red element, 'fire', symbolizing the Han. There is still no certainty about the causes of the rebellion. Investigation of the scanty documents shows that there was no particularly drastic or sudden deterioration in material welfare, which would not necessarily be the case anyway, when the insurgents were motivated by an ideology, a desire for 'justice'. On the contrary, it is very rare for great hardship to give rise to rebellion. The usual response to it is apathetic resignation. Rebellion is most likely to flourish when there are real grounds to hope for improvement, when the oppressed think they can see fissures and rifts in the structure of government. No one should therefore be surprised if the 'demoralization of Han officialdom' (Michaud), that is, the general decline in the power of the government, is associated with the outbreak of revolt. Decline of the state's local power was just the thing to assist development of an organization hostile to the state. The rebellions of this period were the first instance in Chinese history of action by quasi-ecclesiastical societies, whose members were united by chiliastic hopes. The leader of the Yellow Turbans, Chang Chüeh (d. 184), is said to have allowed a rumour to circulate among his followers, which may indicate a deliberate intention to seize power: 'The blue heaven [the Han emperor] is dead, the yellow heaven [as the leader of the Yellow Turbans called himself, in allusion to the mythical Yellow Emperor] will reign.' The revolts have been given other interpretations: that they attempted to contain the influence of the large landowners and prevent a contingent diminution of autonomy among the lower classes, which was small enough anyway and had at least been guaranteed for a time by government from the centre; or that the small farmers were resisting the threat to their way of life represented by the concentration of land in the possession of a few large families (Franke/Trauzettel). At all events, both the central government and the

118

peripheral authorities countered them with the swiftest of action. The Yellow Turbans were effectively routed within a year. The Five Bushels of Rice movement was isolated and surrendered in 215. Their defeat profited not the Han dynasty, but the regional governors appointed to defend their interests, above all Ts'ao Ts'ao (155–220) and his family. Once again popular rebellion contributed to the downfall of a dynasty, while the new governing power emerged from the traditional upper classes, to the discomfiture both of the old dynasty and of the rebels themselves. Their defeat on this occasion by no means disrupted the insurgent tradition; adherents of the Yellow Turbans were still active as late as the fifth century; but above all, right up to the last phase of the imperial era, Popular Taoism remained one of the principal stimuli behind any anti-governmental alliances. None of the protagonists ever realized that the archaic Taoist dream of a return to a primitive society free from state interference was simultaneously one of the principal reasons why the rebellions launched by the conspiracies could never hope to be successful. At a later date, Popular Buddhism also proved a major inspiration of insurgency. One of the earliest uprisings under a Buddhist banner is recorded under the Sui dynasty. In the year 610 about a hundred zealots forced their way into the imperial palace, claiming that the coming of the Bodhisattva Maitreya (*Mi-lo-fo*) had introduced a new era. They were cut down on the spot, but the expectation of a redeemer lived on, and repeatedly inspired rebellions among the ranks of the common people in later centuries.

In the second half of the ninth century, for the first time, a rebel leader took the stage who differed from his predecessors in having first tried to rise to a position of power by the conventional means, that is, by taking the civil service examinations. Huang Ch'ao (d. 884) came from a family that over several generations in the salt trade had amassed a respectable fortune. Huang's attempts to gain the entrée to the educated class failed. He apparently had more aptitude for the martial arts than for reading. Whether it was this natural inclination or the need to safeguard his half-legal, half-illegal business activities that decided him on rebellion, is unclear. What is certain is that as a failed examination candidate he was the prototype of many future rebel leaders. Before Huang Ch'ao and his several thousands of followers even began their more than five-year progress through the empire, from the north down to the south and west, several spontaneous uprisings had occurred in different parts of the realm. Prolonged drought in what is now the province of Honan led to a famine in the year 873 which the decaying central government of the T'ang was incapable of relieving; the local landowning aristocracy, too, did nothing to fundamentally alleviate the hardship. Bands of desperadoes roamed about the countryside pillaging; large sectors of the starving population migrated to other regions. In about 875 a certain Wang Hsien-chih came to prominence as the leader of one of the strongest bands. Huang Ch'ao is said to have supported this band for several years, but there is no reason to suppose that he did so on purely humanitarian grounds. Connections in the 'underworld' would have been very convenient for Huang in his dealings in the salt trade. He certainly seems to have had more than a business relationship with Wang, and eventually became one of his lieutenants. When the T'ang court attempted to buy Wang off with the offer of an official stipend, and Wang was prepared to accept, Huang Ch'ao intervened, since he himself would have gone empty-handed from the arrangement. Wang Hsien-chih was captured and beheaded (878), and Huang Ch'ao assumed the command of the rebel forces. Murdering and plundering, he advanced as far as Canton and the capital, Ch'ang-an. He proclaimed himself emperor and attempted to set up an administrative organization. However, he was forced to fill posts with his own followers, who were often illiterate. He was unable to persuade the officials who had served the T'ang in the areas he had swept through to work for him, and he also failed to win the support of the ordinary people. When he was forced to pull out of Ch'ang-an in 881 he was stoned. In revenge, when he managed to retake the city, he is supposed to have had eighty thousand of the inhabitants put to death. The local farming population fled into the mountains and thus withdrew the rebels' source of supplies; many of them are said to have turned to cannibalism. Finally, in 884 Huang Ch'ao was defeated by Li K'o-yung, a general of Turkish (*Sha-t'o*) descent (d. 908). This ended the insurgency which, for all its origins in a socio-revolutionary situation, had never attempted to reach any socio-revolutionary goals. It had been made possible by the dynasty's decline, which it had hastened yet further. In a sense, one of the movement's participants profited from the situation that it created, though not until he had joined the ranks of the military governors who held the real power at that time. This was Chu Wen (852–912), formerly one of Huang Ch'ao's lieutenants, who had gone over to the emperor's side in 882 in return for an official post. After eliminating his rival Li K'o-yung, Chu Wen founded the first of the short-lived Five Dynasties, the Later Liang dynasty (907–23).

A rebellion on a larger scale, which tied the government down for several years, and so influenced its confrontation with the external enemy, took place in the last years of the Northern Sung. It too was preceded by local unrest and uprisings, before a movement on a national scale got under way, led by one Fang La (d. 1121). The rank and file of the rebels were mostly forced labourers, transportation workers in what is now Chekiang. Fang La, who began to march northwards with a large following in 1120, is said in the official sources to have been an adherent of a heretical faith, possibly Mazdaism. According to other sources, however, he had owned a small craft business, which had been ruthlessly plundered by minor officials seeking to please the emperor. Allegedly, in particular he had been dispossessed by the sycophant Chu Mien (d. 1126), a defence commissioner, who collected every available rarity and curiosity for dispatch to the capital, even if it meant tearing down houses and demolishing walls. Fang La's aim, which also appealed to his followers, was to get rid of all the corrupt officials 'who simply take what they want'. It is significant that this train of embittered, resentful men did not molest officials who had 'governed well'. There can be no doubt that Fang La's revolt was one of those which were directed, not against the system, but against its abuses. There is, however, a trace of racialism in his condemnation not only of the wastefulness of the capital, but also of the payment of immense sums in tribute to the foreign states of Liao-Kitan and Hsi-Hsia-Tangut, which all had to be found 'by us in the south-east', and which only made the foreigners despise China the more. It would not do to make too much of this argument: the bone of contention was not so much that tribute was being paid to foreigners, as that too much was expected of the state's producers. The resistance shown by some sections of the Chinese population, who came under the rule of the Jurchen and later of the Mongols, and rose against their foreign overlords in the thirteenth century, was perhaps a different matter. One 'resistance group', which gave itself the name of 'Loyal Army of Red Jackets' (*Hung-ao chung-i-chün*), was able to hold out for nearly sixty years (1205–62) in a part of Shantung, launching guerilla attacks on the occupying forces. It had connections with the Southern Sung, who sent them financial support from time to time.

The first large-scale insurgent movement to bear an unmistakable

121

ethnic, 'nationalist' trait arose towards the end of the Mongols' rule. The internal disputes which increasingly weakened the Mongol government from the beginning of the fourteenth century onwards have already been mentioned; likewise the bitter resentment in southern and central China of the social categorization imposed by the Mongols. When famine spread through large areas of north China in the 1330s, and floods made the population homeless, people living north of the Huaiho were also ready to join anti-dynastic movements. The nuclei of these movements were generally religious or semi-religious secret societies. As always, opposition to the government had to start underground, only coming into the open when central and local government had grown weak and the population were already on the move. The best-known sect of this period was the 'White Lotus Society' (*Pai-lien-hui*), who originated from the Buddhist T'ien-t'ai sect of the sixth century. As in the case of the Yellow Turbans, its leader nourished their followers' messianic expectations, and exhorted them to prepare for the coming upheaval. They announced the imminent coming of the Bodhisattva Maitreya, the Buddha of the future, whose advent had already been proclaimed at the beginning of the seventh century. Chu Yüan-chang (1328–98), the founder of the Ming dynasty, grew up against the background of one of these secret societies. It is not clear from the sources whether he was actually a member or not. Certainly, once he had ascended the throne it would have been against his interests to admit to such an affiliation and thereby appear to sanction what was always in principle a subversive organization. When he had become emperor, he singled out the White Lotus, condemning its rites as absurd and designed to mislead the people. Yet his own history suggests that he was more likely to have been connected with the White Lotus than any other society. When he was orphaned at the age of seventeen, he entered a Buddhist monastery, where he learned to read and write. At twenty-five he joined a band of robbers, led by a soothsayer, Kuo Tzu-hsing (c. 1352). Within the space of a few years he had collected followers of his own, with whose help he soon won a prominent position in the region (now Anhui), torn as it was by numerous rebel movements. In 1356 he left his base in his homeland and conquered Nanking. He spent the next ten years building up an independent regime in the wealthy, fertile Yangtse valley, complete with local administration and military organization. He succeeded in so far as he managed to gain the support of the wealthy and educated classes. This was only possible because his movement had taken on a distinct anti-Mongol character as time passed, and had lost its aspirations to social reform. In this way, he had managed by 1367 to eliminate his most important rivals. In 1368 his troops took the Mongol capital, Ta-tu (Peking), and in the same year, with the help of his learned advisers, Chu Yüan-chang founded the Ming dynasty. His success confirmed the transfer of the mandate of heaven. There are only two other rebel leaders of humble origins in the whole course of Chinese history who have had comparable success: Liu Pang, the founder of the Han dynasty, and – if it is not still too early to draw the comparison – Mao Tse-tung. Chu Yüan-chang has often been criticized for his collaboration with the traditional elite, his abandonment of the social goals he had originally professed, and his transformation into a conservative emperor, for whom 'reasons of state' were the highest political principles.

The criticism is not altogether just. It is true that he introduced no social change in the sense of a revolution, but he did stabilize the way of life of the mass of the population, he did restore a properly administered government and, as a by-product of that, he did relieve the burdens of the common people. In the context of traditional China that was a social reform in itself. Whether fundamental social changes could have reduced the latent antagonism between the governing class and the governed, is an open question.

There were no fundamental social changes, and no 'new men'. Consequently similar circumstances came into being towards the end of the Ming dynasty as had existed at the end of the Yüan. Administrative breakdown, corruption and despotism on the part of local potentates, whether holding official appointments or not, and the hardship this produced for the ordinary people, had long been getting worse. The historian Chao I (1727–1814) described the development, which was by no means unique to the Ming period, in the following terms:

In general it was the case under the late Ming dynasty that the people were not only taxed out of existence by the local officials on numerous illegal pretexts, but were also regarded as easy prey by most of the members of the educated class who lived in the country but did not hold official posts ["Gentry"], and who took advantage of their connections and their privileged rank. Officials above and privileged non-officials below protected and covered up for each other.

123

When a series of natural disasters in the late 1620s led to famine in the province of Shensi and there was no reduction in taxes, unrest grew which soon spread to the neighbouring provinces. The disturbances became revolt when the Ming administration was forced to give its full attention to the Manchu invasion in the north and two ambitious leaders, both with a talent for organization, took command. Li Tzu-ch'eng (c. 1605–45) and Chang Hsien-chung (1605–47) were both natives of Shensi and both had belonged to outlaw bands for years. Li succeeded in conquering the whole of north China within a few years. From about 1640 onwards he tried to build up an administration in his hinterland with the help of some educated advisers, but the military situation made it virtually impossible. It is worthy of note that it was Li's advisers who were concerned to build him up systematically as a leader, including the creation of a public image. At the same time they tried to exercise a moral influence over him. They recommended him to distribute food to sections of the population in desperate need. But Li does not seem to have worried very much about laying firm foundations in local support. Scarcely had he proclaimed his new Shun dynasty (1643) than he advanced on Peking, driving the last Ming emperor to suicide. On the whole it seems that conditions were not unfavourable for Li's putsch to have succeeded, but, as almost always in situations of that kind, he was not the only one to aspire to the supreme power. His rival Chang Hsien-chung had also set up a 'central government' on the Ming pattern with the aid of educated advisers, at first in north China and then retrenched in Ssechuan. In the end both were wiped out very quickly by Wu San-kuei (1612–78), formerly the Ming frontier commander, who had made common cause with the Manchu.

The revolts led by Li Tzu-ch'eng and Chang Hsien-chung were only the most prominent of the uprisings in the first half of the seventeenth century. In addition, the White Lotus sect was active in Shantung in the 1620s, though their influence remained purely local. The tradition lived on, even after the suppression of the uprisings in Shantung, for in the late eighteenth century the first large-scale politico-social rising for nearly a hundred years took place in their name. The epicentre of this new social disturbance was in the frontier regions of Hupei, Shensi and Ssechuan, where many new communities had been founded during the course of the eighteenth century by migrants from the overcrowded plains of the Huangho and Huaiho, the heartlands of earlier actions by the White Lotus. Regions on the administrative frontiers, that is, the border areas of provinces, had always been the favoured refuges of outlaws and potential rebels, not least because the effective power of the authorities hardly stretched so far. Both the central and the provincial governments had failed to place the new communities firmly under state control. On the other hand the settlers were forever receiving increased demands from tax collectors who were also not under state control. The administrative vacuum was quite extraordinarily favourable to the formation of resistance movements. Members of the White Lotus Society provided the organization. Within a few years they stirred large numbers of the settlers in the border regions to rise in protest against, primarily, the extortionate tax collectors and the growing influence of the authorities. The leader of the White Lotus revival was taken prisoner and banished to the frontier at an early stage, but his successors retained control over his followers. They now declared a political goal: the deposition of the Ch'ing dynasty. They proclaimed a boy from Hunan as the successor of the Ming and rose in open rebellion. The second generation of leaders were also removed from the scene and the authorities persecuted the population wholesale, without regard to guilt or innocence. They did so not least at the behest of the greedy and ambitious minister Ho-shen (1750–99). The result was that, though it now lacked centralized leadership, the revolt spread into the heart of the provinces of Hupei, Shensi and Ssechuan, and into the neighbouring provinces of Kansu and Honan. The rebels' slogan was 'The officials have driven the people to rise.' The same slogan figures in the novel *All Men are Brothers* (*Shui-hu chuan*), about an episode in the Sung period, in which it is used to justify the actions of bandits and rebels. The Ch'ing government was compelled to dispatch full-scale military expeditions to put down the insurgents. The troops were, however, so badly organized and supplied and so ill-disciplined that it took them nearly nine years (1796–1804) to quell the poorly equipped, and for the most part isolated, bands of rebels.

Barely ten years later the Ch'ing had another rebellion on their hands, with a militant core of members of two secret societies practising magic and religious ceremonials, which had sprung from the White Lotus sect. These, the 'Eight Trigrams' (*Pa-kua-chiao*) and the 'Heavenly Principle' (*T'ien-li-chiao*), operated primarily in north-east China and were suppressed with relative ease by the central government (1813). But by this time the secret societies had been long established as the nuclei around which political opposition from the

125

lower classes could crystallize. This applied even if it had not been an essential attribute at the time of their foundation. Since opposition to the *status quo* could not be freely expressed, secret societies, even those founded originally for quite different motives, were the only possible vehicle for protest. Even the Christian communities were regarded as dangerous secret organizations, from the point of view of the government, and they were persecuted from time to time. There was also a ramifying group of secret societies in south China, known variously as the 'Triad Society' (*San-ho-hui*), 'Heaven and Earth Society' (*T'ien-ti-hui*) or the 'Hung League' (*Hung-meng*). Its members came mostly from the mobile sections of the population, such as transportation workers, merchants, showmen and emigrants – there are supposed to be many adherents of the society even today among the Chinese population of south-east Asia. According to their tradition, which went back to a Buddhist monk of the seventeenth century, they were opposed to the Ch'ing regime and loyal to the Ming. This principle had fallen somewhat into abeyance in the eighteenth century, and the society had become essentially nothing more than an organization for mutual protection and profit-making. One indication of this is that by the early nineteenth century its members rarely involved themselves in open rebellion; in practice, only when they fell foul of the state through their occasionally criminal activities.

As the organs of government lost effective administrative control and ceased to maintain stability in the country's economy, which meant in the last resort restraining local potentates without official appointments, so it was possible for secret societies to take *de facto* control locally, and occasionally even regionally, collecting taxes, recruiting labour and administering justice. This was particularly the case in eastern and central parts of south China (Kuangtung, Kuangsi and Hunan), where circumstances particularly favourable to the secret societies evolved during the 1840s. The Opium War had struck the prestige and self-reliance of the governing class an especially heavy blow in that part of the country. As a consequence of the treaty of 1843, overseas trade had been transferred to Shanghai. Thousands of transportation workers and traders who lived along the inland route to Canton, previously the only legal entrepôt, suddenly lost their livelihood. Additionally, the British had driven the smugglers, who were sometimes pirates as well, out of the waters along the south-east coast, and they had taken refuge either on the mainland or on the more remote islands such as Taiwan. With large numbers of malcontents and people who had been uprooted from their homes, it needed only an inflammatory idea and a compelling leader to set the whole situation ablaze. A leader was to hand, in Hung Hsiu-ch'üan (1814–64). Hung was a failed examination candidate like Huang Ch'ao; he had had superficial contacts with Christianity. He is supposed to have been told in a vision, while he was ill, that he was Christ's younger brother and that it was his task to save the world. Hung came from a Hakka family who farmed in Kuangtung. The Hakkas ('guest families') had migrated from north China in the first millennium and settled in the coastal areas of the south-east. There they remained largely isolated from the Punti ('natives') by language and customs. Many Hakkas had long before left the hostile environment in Kuangtung, even after their ancestors had lived there for centuries, and migrated to the poorer, but less densely populated border regions of Kuangsi. It was among these people that Hung and his friends began their proselytizing for the 'Society of the Worshippers of God' (*Pai-shang-ti-hui*). Significantly they met with little response from the farmers at first: their recruits were mainly foresters, miners, transportation workers, ex-soldiers, pirates and smugglers. As the new converts, in their zeal, began to destroy Chinese shrines, which they regarded as the work of devils, the authorities intervened. A lieutenant of the sect was taken prisoner: the 'Worshippers' released him and in so doing openly defied the state; the movement was now an insurrection. There was only one way open to them, in the circumstances, to avoid certain extermination: to take the offensive. Several quick successes strengthened the rebels in their belief. As early as 1851 Hung Hsiu-ch'üan proclaimed the 'Heavenly Kingdom of Great Peace' (*T'ai-p'ing t'ien-kuo*). A comprehensive programme was drawn up, based in part on earlier tracts by Hung and in part on newly formulated ideas that were an amalgam of Christian, Taoist and Buddhist elements and even a sprinkling of Confucianism. In some of its aspirations the Taiping programme was genuinely revolutionary. Monotheism was the basic premiss and the idea of equality evolved from that. There should be no more private ownership of land; occupiers of holdings should enjoy the usufruct only; there should be equality of the sexes; concubinage was to be abolished. There were, however, not only contradictions in the way the system was put into practice – the leaders of the movement claimed privileges of their own – but it was riddled with contradictions in itself. For instance, the egalitarian principle conflicted with retention of the traditional norms governing the hierarchy of human relationships. The Confucians in

127

particular had always urged maintenance of these values, namely the morally distinct obligations of ruler and official (*chün-ch'en*), father and son (*fu-tzu*), husband and wife (*fu-fu*), older and younger brothers (*hsiung-ti*), older and younger friends (*p'eng-yu*).

After announcing their bid for power the Taiping overran the province of Hunan in a few months and struck down the Yangtse to Nanking, which they took in 1853 and made their capital. Other offensives were launched from there, as far as Tientsin and Shansi among other places. But there was little coordination in these undertakings and they were essentially hardly more than looting forays. The rebels did not make adequate provision to ensure their hold on the hinterland they had marched through and reconstruction was only undertaken in the immediate vicinity of Nanking. The Taiping control of the greater part of southern and central China was largely a cartographical figment, a factor which assisted their opponents in organizing counter-measures. They met with opposition in various quarters. Naturally the court could not allow any other body to assume its prerogative of 'the legitimate use of physical force' (Max Weber). But that all of the upper classes, including the civil service, should support the foreign rulers rather than the native rebels, was less predictable, given the precedent of Chu Yüan-chang's overthrow of the Mongol dynasty. They certainly regarded rebels by definition as lawbreakers, but in times of crisis the definition had always been relative. They were more strongly influenced by the fact that the beliefs of the Taiping questioned very nearly the whole hierarchy of traditional values. In addition they feared for their possessions under the Taiping social and economic programme. The same apprehension also alienated the smaller landowners. The Taiping also aroused the hostility of the poor among the settled rural population. They still had their gods and demons to lose; they were probably more offended than the upper classes by the religious fanaticism and puritanism of the Taiping. Finally the Europeans in China, who had hoped at first that they would be able to make more favourable arrangements with a 'Christian' China, turned against them when they realized the Taiping had no intention of honouring their special privileges.

An official, Tseng Kuo-fan (1811–72), began to organize a force in 1852, which gradually gained experience in combating the rebels and eventually, with the aid of the units specially formed by Li Hung-chang (1823–1901) and Tso Tsung-t'ang (1812–85) and the Ever Victorious Army led by English and French officers, crushed the Taiping in 1864.

Some of the reasons why the movement alienated the most important strata of Chinese society have already been mentioned; so too its
tactical weaknesses. But its defeat was also due to other factors. The
Taiping failed, and repeatedly refused, to make common cause with
other insurgent groups, not least the widespread Triad Society. Both
the leadership and the rank and file were torn by regional and factional
jealousies; for the whole of the time after the taking of Nanking a
suicidal struggle for power raged at the top. The movement which
might have set China on a new road turned into a Gadarene rout.

The political consequences of the Taiping rebellion should not be
underestimated, however. After its defeats in the Opium War (1839–42)
and the War of 1856–58 (the Lorcha War), the Manchu central government had now demonstrated its growing weakness in internal affairs.
It was obvious that real power was transferring itself to the periphery
again, into the hands of high-ranking Chinese officials. Above all,
however, the wind raised by the major rebellion also created a kind of
leeside, in which minor revolts elsewhere broke out, so that in the end
hardly a province in the empire was spared disturbance. Chinese
Moslems revolted in the south-western and north-western provinces of
Yünnan, Shensi and Kansu and in Turkestan (1855–78) and the Miao
ethnic minority rose in Kueichou (1854–73). But the principal rebellion
to take fire from the Taiping was the Nien revolt in north China
(1853–68).

The Nien secret societies had already existed for a considerable time
in the border areas of the provinces of Shantung, Kiangsu, Honan and
Anhui. Some of them were religious groups with connections with the
White Lotus of the earlier part of the century. Others, however, were
local gangs thrown together by their lot, such as hoodlums, gamblers
and smugglers. It is certainly no accident that the salt-trader Chang
Lo-hsing (d. 1863) succeeded in coordinating a large number of
isolated local bands at the very moment when the Taiping were at the
height of their success, and when large areas of the land between the
Huangho and the Huaiho had been flooded (1853). They had their
first clash with the government in the same year and the movement
became a revolt. Several hundreds of local bands under local leaders,
including some from the rural landowning class, took over the
administration of their neighbourhoods. Chang's coordination failed
to get all the units to act together; the leaders of the Nien were
incapable of more far-reaching ambition. The rebellion only took on a
certain tinge of revolutionary politics after splinter groups left the

129

Taiping and joined Nien units (1863–64), but by then it was already too late. After defeating the Taiping Tseng Kuo-fan and later Li Hung-chang turned their attention to wiping out the Nien. The state gradually encroached on the administrative vacuum, and, using traditional methods of encirclement, attrition, isolation and infiltration, Li sealed the last stragglers in a trap from which guerilla action was impossible, and then 'pacified' them (1868). Significantly the local population submitted to the authorities' 'pacification' as readily as they had joined the rebels. They always supported the force that offered them the greatest chance of peace and security.

On the surface, 'internal unrest' (*nei-yu*) seemed to have died down by the late 1870s. The court and the civil service believed that they could devote their energies entirely to the 'external aggression' (*wai-luan*). But since only a superficial solution had been found to the internal problems, while external aggression still increased, unrest and bitterness continued to seethe among the population. It boiled over at last in one more rebellion, the last traditional rising and simultaneously the first directed specifically against the foreigners from across the seas. Another, probably unique, feature was the court's manipulation of the movement to its own ends. The revolt became known as the Boxer Rising. The 'Fists of Justice and Harmony' (*I-ho-ch'üan*) were branches of the Eight Trigram Society, and thus belonged to the White Lotus alliance. Like many other sects of basically religious inspiration they believed themselves called to combat the 'devils' in the world. They had no other more specific or rational goals. They firmly believed that they would be able to drive out the devils with magic powers. At first the non-Chinese Manchu were their devils. Their slogan was 'Down with the Ch'ing, bring back the Ming.' But eventually they turned more and more against the non-Asiatic foreigners and their unwelcome modernistic ways. Their spontaneous, fanatical acts were directed first and foremost against the material innovations introduced and generally administered by the foreigners, but also against the propagandists of 'devilish' ideas, the missionaries. The material innovations had led to changes that caused great hardship in particular quarters: large numbers of transportation workers, for instance, had lost their livelihood with the building of railways. The notions spread by the missionaries, who were beyond the pale of the law, would pervert the true order of the world and lead the people of China astray, or so the Boxers believed. The immediate consequence of their actions was that the foreign powers claimed reparations from the Chinese

130

government and demanded suppression of the Boxers. The authorities found it hard to disband them, and probably they had some sympathy with them, at least for those of their activities that were directed against the foreigners. The Manchu governor of Shantung, Yü-hsien (d. 1901), far from disbanding them, formed them into militia units, with the new slogan of 'Support the Ch'ing, down with the foreigners from overseas' (1899). This was only the beginning of the recruitment of these undisciplined zealots in the service of the state, and demonstrates the desolate situation in which the dynasty found itself. Influential court circles close to the Empress Dowager Tzu-hsi (1835–1908) looked on the Boxers as a force that could be used to the advantage of the conservative faction over against the reformers who had just been dismissed. They even nurtured the hope that the Boxers would be able to drive the 'barbarians' out of China, if they actually possessed the spiritual strength that they claimed, or that at the very least the rest of the population would also rise against the foreigners. At the invitation of these circles at the court the Boxers entered Peking. After various incidents they besieged the legation quarter of the city (20 June to 14 August 1900), while the court, believing that it had the whole of China behind it, declared war on the foreign powers (21 June 1900). The powers sent an expeditionary force which took Peking after a few weeks. The court was forced to flee to one of the parts of China which had been kept out of the confrontation by the regional governors. Nearly all the governors had left the dynasty in the lurch; from a strictly legal point of view they had not been at war with the foreign powers at all. The Boxers, who had never had proper leadership, were done for, both as a Citizen Army acting for the dynasty and as a popular insurgent movement. Their rising nevertheless had serious consequences, not only for the court but also for China as a whole. The real power now lay completely in the hands of the regional governors; the foreign influences grew out of all proportions, and the terms of the Boxer Protocol subjected the Chinese people to new, heavy burdens.

The end of the traditional Chinese state meant also the end of its correlative, the traditional insurgent movement. Each had conditioned the other for over two thousand years; neither was suited to a changed world. Secret societies were not to be the places where alternative ways of distributing power were thought up in the next fifty years. That function, and the political expression of social and economic dissatisfaction were taken over by political parties. The first of the new parties, which is still in existence, the Nationalist Party of China

131

(*Kuo-min-tang*), was already in the process of forming by 1900. Sun Yat-sen (1866–1925) gave it a programme including, for the first time, an institutional alternative to the traditional relationship between the rulers and the ruled. Even so, this new beginning was still rooted in the tradition of the secret societies and insurgent movements, and was only a preparatory stage in the total reshaping of Chinese society.

Obviously, in the present context it has been impossible to mention more than a handful of the literally hundreds of insurrections and rebellions in Chinese history. It must be said that at virtually every period various conditions existed in which the lower classes of traditional Chinese society might decide to resist their rulers. Wolfram Eberhard has worked out the pattern of the genesis of a rebellion, starting with one of these typical sets of circumstances, and his pattern is reproduced here in a condensed form.

In a homogeneous cell of society, such as a village, certain men or youths take on specific watch and guard duties in their spare time. They form a band, which comes to compete with similar groups from other villages. Various provocative acts take place, such as diverting a watercourse to the benefit of their own village. If pressure is put on the village through natural catastrophes or official or semi-official demands, the band acts as provider and protector, by robbing the rich or chasing away the tax collectors. If these people belong to the upper classes or the civil service, or if they have influence with the authorities, a confrontation may take place between the band and the arm of the state. If they resist the 'bandits' are branded as 'rebels'. To escape capture they are forced to withdraw into regions on the fringes of the administration's reach, into the mountains or out to sea. During the first stage of the rebellion they maintain their contacts with the village. The village provides for the rebels' wants, and they protect the village in return. They enlarge the source of their provisions by raids in the neighbourhood. If fugitives and vagrants swell the numbers of the band, the source of provisions must be further enlarged. They come into conflict with neighbouring bands, who lose 'their' villages to the victors if they are beaten. The state, the authorities and the classes of society affiliated to them become alarmed and send the military against the rebels. There is fighting outside the larger villages and towns. If the rebels win their numbers are augmented by deserters from the army. At this stage the educated and landowning classes are in a considerable dilemma. If they yield to the rebels' pressure and give them support, they will have to answer to the old authority when and

132

if the rebels are defeated. The rebels are forced to conquer new territory in order to secure provision for their ever-growing numbers and to satisfy their expectations of loot. In order to secure the territories that they overrun the rebels need the collaboration of the administrative specialists of the upper classes. If they fail to win their support the rebellion is as good as doomed. If the leaders of the rebellion insinuate themselves into the upper classes and so win the support they need, the mass of their followers find themselves once again under upper-class control. Once that stage is reached, the rebellion has been disarmed from the point of view of the rulers, and from the point of view of the ruled it has failed.

The only changes ever brought about by any of the rebellions were, as has been shown, in the persons holding power, not in the institutions of power and certainly not in the structure of society. Some of the rebel leaders seem, indeed, to have had no other purpose in mind. Their risings were a means of seizing 'legal' power, or, if they allowed themselves to be bought off handsomely enough, a means of access to power. The 'stupid (common) people' (*yü-min*), with no means of articulating their discontent and despair other than uncoordinated, spontaneous uprisings, benefited to only a limited degree from the rebellions stirred up in their name. Economic hardship, judicial discrimination and natural catastrophes were frequently factors in the launching of rebellion, but not necessarily among the leaders' motives. Poverty and hardship fuelled insurrectionary movements, just as religious propaganda stirred up enthusiasm and extremism. The fact remains that the material factors inciting to rebellion were allowed to recur with frightening regularity.

The leaders of rebel bands rarely came from the very lowest ranks of society. Most of them were 'semi-educated' (*pan-sheng pu-shu*) examination candidates (Huang Ch'ao, Hung Hsiu-ch'üan), minor officials (Liu Pang), smugglers (Chang Hsien-chung, Chang Lo-hsing), monks (Chu Yüan-chang), priests (Chang Chüeh), soothsayers (Kuo Tzu-hsing) – men with at least a rudimentary education. The fact that not one of them ever developed a genuine alternative, new patterns of thought and society, is due to a basic acceptance by every Chinese of the traditional order of things. Rulers and ruled obeyed the same law. Both sectors of society saw the world as subject to a moral order, dominated by the principle that just rewards were meted out in this life, and sanctioned ultimately by heaven itself. There was no fundamental distinction between the ideologies of the

133

rulers and the ruled, even if the rulers were always insisting that it was the heterodox beliefs of such cults as Maitreya Buddhism or Popular Taoism that led the masses astray and stirred up revolt.

Although the characteristics of insurrection and rebellion in China do display a certain consistency when presented in this fashion, there is simultaneously a shift of emphasis to be observed in the long term. Egalitarian aims, for instance, were expressly formulated for the first time in the middle of the T'ang period, due perhaps to changes in socio-economic circumstances and a resulting increase in social mobility (Muramatsu Yuji). Possibly it was the state itself, in its attempts to create fairer economic conditions by such means as the Equal Field System or the Double Tax System, that fostered the notion that land could be more equally distributed. From the Later T'ang onwards resistance was increasingly directed only secondarily against the central government. Its immediate object was the steadily strengthening position of the educated and wealthy elite and bureaucracy at local levels. It is characteristic, too, that from this time, as commerce became more and more important in the Chinese economy, merchants and traders of all kinds were more frequently found at the head of insurgent groups. It must be reiterated that this class always operated on the fringes of legality, especially in the realm of the state monopolies. But even when their business was wholly legitimate they were always particularly liable to obstruction by officials, who as a class were anti-commercial. Another nuance was added in the Sung period with the rise of an ethnically based nationalism. The reasons for it are obvious. From that time onwards large areas of the territories settled by Han Chinese fell repeatedly to foreign conquerors, some of whom interfered considerably with the institutions and rights of the Chinese population.

Thus the political articulation of the common people, the insurrectionary movements, remained rooted in the overall context of historical development. In other words, any changes in the nature of them followed and influenced changes in the political articulation of the governing class, the superstructure of the state. Both were interdependent aspects of one and the same tradition.

CHINA AND THE OUTSIDE WORLD

China's attitude to the world outside has always been, and still is, of particular interest to the non-Chinese observer. The question as to whether she is potentially an aggressive expansionist or always acts defensively only is one to which the past will provide answers either way. Assessment of the past is clearly not simple, otherwise it would be impossible to reconcile the interpretation of purely military advances into central Asia, as under the Han or the T'ang, as merely defensive acts, on the one hand, while on the other the essentially peaceful exaction of tribute from numerous 'vassal' states almost throughout Chinese history is interpreted as hegemonial ambition. There is, however, less dispute nowadays about the genesis of the ethnic, cultural and political unit that is called China. The assumption that China, at least in the early epochs, arose from a largely independent, autochthonous development, and that she neutralized subsequent alien influences has been superseded. There is general agreement that, from its beginnings, the civilization that became known as Chinese was the product of a complex ethnic and cultural synthesis, and also that imperial China absorbed some essential formative influences from outside. One of the most important forces in China's history is the interaction of the ethnic, political and cultural currents. Sometimes they ebbed out of China, and sometimes they flowed with equal strength from outside. Within the field of tension they set up, 'Chinese' civilization fought to assert itself as an organized entity, eventually emerging in its distinctive form.

Despite the contacts existing over millennia between China and the more or less organized polities on her borders, a number of reputable authorities maintain that until the last phase, the nineteenth century, traditional China had no external policies. They assert that instead, China merely projected outwards the precepts governing her internal affairs, seeing every foreign neighbour as a potential addition to herself (W. Franke). This view may seem surprising on the face of it, but it is not without justification. At no stage did monarchic China ever have either a Foreign Ministry or, terminologically, 'foreign relations'. References in the sources to China's relationships with external powers are so fragmentary as often to be barely recognizable as such. Alternatively they are concealed in the terminology of frontier controls, frontier trade, delegations bringing tribute, ceremonies, military strategy. But in practice even historical China clearly distinguished internal from external affairs. There was even formal machinery for communicating with other states, such as the tribute system which had a double orientation in accordance with its dual nature. The system regulated both internal and external relations, and although it bore no resemblance to modern European processes, it nevertheless performed a comparable function so far as foreign policy was concerned. The origins of the system lie in the Chou period. During this time the Central Plains, the nucleus of later China, was occupied by several related communities, of various sizes, whose relationships with each other were closer than those of separate states. Their relationships were essentially a matter of internal affairs, though they were by no means always peaceful. In general, the communities acknowledged the unity of their culture and life style. From a very early date this set them apart from the world of 'others', of 'barbarians', that lay all round them and even between some of the individual states. The area occupied by Chinese culture was 'fenced in' (Freyer), at first in order to exclude all those who had not made the same advances, and then to exclude the neighbours who were related culturally. Both kinds of exclusion can be observed coming into force under the Chou simultaneously. A specific kind of alliance grew up between the related communities, with features of both an internal and an external relationship. The distinction between their attitudes to each other and to outsiders grew fainter under the empire but never dissolved altogether. Countries like Korea or its predecessors, the Liu-ch'iu islands and a series of other organized social entities, for many centuries occupied a special position by comparison with the rest of the world. Where ritual and cultural affinities persisted, foreign societies belonged to an inner circle and exclusively enjoyed a special relationship with China. The Us and Them distinction only becomes obscure in so far as the same means of formal communication was often employed for both the inner circle and the world beyond. Even so there was a substantial qualification, as will be shown.

The distinction between the inner circle and the outside world did not, however, primarily result from ritual and cultural differences. It was based first and foremost on the differences in political organization and production methods. It is significant that, from the middle of the Chou period onwards, if not earlier, the distinctions were not regarded as insuperable or racially fixed. All aliens, all 'barbarians' could, in theory, become participants in the central 'Chinese' civilization, providing they wholeheartedly adopted its principles, its way of life, in short, the 'right way' (*tao*). According to the Confucian idea of sovereignty, the ruler might win the world to turn to China and be converted to the Chinese way of life, which alone was true civilization (*hua*), without needing to use force, by the mere strength of his moral

136

radiance (*te*). This thesis, which became state dogma under the empire, like most other Confucian postulates, has been interpreted by some European commentators as evidence of a Chinese-Confucian pacifism (Tomkinson). If alien races did not submit themselves, the ruler of China had to prove that he possessed such civilized qualities and such a noble character that he won their hearts instead. The thesis was never anything but a theory, unsubstantiated by events. But that has not hindered historiographical apologists in China, right up to the present day, from energetically working to demonstrate its truth. This suggests that the theory did more to stabilize internal power relationships than to describe actual political situations. It is also apposite to point out that the virtue of yielding and giving in to others (*jang*), lauded by Confucians and Taoists alike, was in only a limited sense courtesy or even altruism. In its origins at least, it was far more of a mystical ritual intended to ensure the attainment of the goal in question (Granet).

What was later to regard itself as the Chinese world reached the two most important frontiers of its traditional homeland at an early stage in its history: the agricultural frontier in the north and the mainland coast in the east. The confrontation in the north between a settled, agrarian society and a nomadic society was one of the most important constants in the whole of China's history until the most recent past. The limit that the ocean imposed on life and mobility, the barrier that it represented, at first, to the further spread of the concept of China as the centre of the world, acquired such a transcending significance, that it was carried over to the land frontiers, in as much as the regions that surrounded the civilized, that is, the sinized world, were known by the term 'the Four Oceans' (*ssu-hai*). 'Barbarians' enclosed the civilized 'island' of China on one side as the sea did on the other. The region of the maritime frontier became another arena for a decisive confrontation, albeit not until the middle of the second millennium AD, for it was above all along the coast that China came face to face with the other major culture that did not conform to hers, with the industrial civilization of the West. The southern frontier of China presented no such drastic cultural confrontation as the north and east. Most peoples on this frontier in historical times lived settled lives, like the inhabitants of the Central Plains. The innate civilizing influence of all higher cultures over races and communities with a different life style, or alternatively, the imposition of their own institutions, was relatively easy there. Some of the southern states, like Ch'u, Wu and

Yüeh, had conformed to the pattern of the principalities of the Central Plains at a very early date. When they became part of the unified empire towards the end of the first millennium BC, they were still regarded for a long time as the exotic south, but not as a foreign territory. While the steppes and deserts of central Asia never became truly Chinese, in the sense of being agriculturally assimilated, the fertile south, already partly under cultivation, proved ideally suited to Chinese expansion. For reasons of agricultural geography, therefore, the traditional northern frontier of China can be regarded as static and exclusive, the old southern frontier, on the other hand, as dynamic and inclusive.

The sense of identity derived from contacts and confrontation with the 'barbarians' whose economy, way of life and social and political organization all differed from those of the Chinese, led in time to an ever stronger consciousness of community, which threw the Us–Them stereotype (*nei-wai*) into ever greater relief. To begin with, however, this consciousness probably formed mainly among the upper classes. When the Chinese script is described as a bond that created and maintained unity, it is obvious that that could apply only to the educated, that is, to the upper, classes. Unity was an ideological pattern imposed from above, both in the early days and under the empire. The mass of the population lacked any horizontal medium of communication, either physical or linguistic. They lived their lives in constricted cells, completely isolated from any but the most immediate locality and with no wider consciousness. But even they grew increasingly aware of a distinction between themselves and the alien complex to the north, not least because of the nomads' southward incursions. It is hard to say when the two levels of consciousness become one; arguably it was not until the second millennium AD, when the whole Chinese world was overrun by an alien, nomadic race. On the other hand, differences between China and the 'barbarians' were permanently smoothed away. Partly this was because the social and political forms of the higher central culture were adopted by its neighbours, as, for example, with Ch'u in the Chou period. It was also partly because these forms were carried along in the wake of Chinese expansionism and imposed on newly taken territories, as in the colonization of south China. Furthermore, ethnic minorities became so closely assimilated to the central tradition, that in the end there was nothing to distinguish them culturally, as in the case of the Manchu. There was, too, at every period, except perhaps under the Ming and the Ch'ing, a lively two-

138

sided exchange of goods and ideas between China and the outside world. While not sufficiently systematic to produce anything like general cultural assimilation, it was nevertheless capable of important results in individual cases. One example of an idea from outside taking root in China is the superseding of the clumsy war chariot by cavalry in the fifth century BC, adopted from the equestrian tribes of central Asia as an efficient means of repelling swift-moving enemies. The reception and spread of Buddhism in China is another comparable event. For her part China radiated so powerful a material and conceptual influence on the surrounding countries of east Asia that its traces are still clearly discernible today, in Japan for instance. Significantly it was not uncommon for Chinese ideas and discoveries to be carried abroad by political refugees. One of the sagas surrounding the origins of Korea, for example, attributes the foundation of the state to a certain Chi-tzu (Kija), a scion of the Shang who is supposed to have refused to serve the Chou after their victory and to have chosen exile among uncivilized aliens instead. There were hundreds of cases under the empire of political emigrants who fled to 'barbarian' tribes in the north or to the offshore islands to the east and there created some at least of the conditions which then made it possible for those tribes to confront China successfully. The prime examples of this were the Liao, Chin, Yüan and Ch'ing dynasties, all of whom originated as northern aliens.

The contacts between China and her neighbours were not exclusively belligerent, despite the antagonism between their cultures, nor were they always explicitly hierarchic. It is recorded that in 318 BC five princes of the Central Plains made an alliance with the Hsiung-nu, a tribe of east Asian Huns, in order to contain the growth in the power of Ch'in. Emperor Han Kao-tsu tried to win friendship with the Hsiung-nu by offering their prince the hand of a Chinese princess in marriage. Han Wu-ti twice sent Chang Ch'ien, a court official, to central Asian neighbours of the Hsiung-nu (Yüeh-chih in Bactria, 139–126 BC; Wu-sun in the Ili valley, 115 BC), in order to mobilize them against the common enemy. Emperor Kuang-wu of the Later Han settled groups of the southern Hsiung-nu along the north Chinese frontier to defend it. The types of contact illustrated by these examples – alliance with external powers in order to influence internal conflicts, conciliating foreign powers by offers of a material or personal kind, mobilization of one 'barbarian' against another, purchasing stability with the concession of land for settlement and reduction of their own freedom to expand – remained among the instruments of foreign policy used by successive dynasties to the end of the empire. This was particularly, but not exclusively, the case when their military superiority and therefore their dominance were in doubt.

The ambassador Chang Ch'ien is reckoned one of the first of China's great travellers. Through him the earliest written reports of the great realm in the far west that the Chinese called Ta-ch'in and the peoples of the Mediterranean called Imperium Romanum, reached the court of a Chinese dynasty. China also got to hear about India and Persia. Quantities of exotic goods arrived in the capital, Ch'ang-an; artistic ideas like the 'Scythian' type of animal figure and new modes of thought like Buddhism gradually infiltrated the country. But politically and ideologically these contacts, especially those with the far west, had no immediate effects. The distances between the eastern and western centres of civilization were too great, the exposed areas where they could make contact were minimal. Nevertheless, in the field of international relations as in so many others, the Han period saw the introduction of some of the most important developments in Chinese history. Not only did central and western Asia advance into unprecedented political prominence in the Chinese view of the world, but news also came from across the maritime frontier of other worlds to the north and the extreme south. There were contacts with the Japanese archipelago from the time of Han Wu-ti's attack on the Korean peninsula, and the outposts on the Tongking and Pearl River deltas stretched out fingers to south-east Asia and southern India, possibly even as far as the Levant. In the early years of the Later Han a Chinese emissary reached the Persian Gulf. The world had become a much larger place from the Chinese viewpoint, within a relatively short time, without China's new knowledge making any qualitative changes in the national self-concept. Quite the reverse: the experience gathered at close quarters and the ideas based upon it were projected into the larger sphere. The definition of 'barbarian', no longer applicable to the areas which had now been largely assimilated into China, was simply transferred to the world beyond, at successively greater removes.

The Hsiung-nu were once again instrumental in the Han downfall. The support of the tribes who had settled within the Great Wall assisted Ts'ao Ts'ao (AD 155–220) to build up his own power on the periphery and make a puppet of the central authority. Similarly, a Chin aspirant to the throne in 304 used Hsiung-nu help in his bid for power; his plan appeared successful, until the Hsiung-nu rose against the Chin and drove them out of their heartland on the Huangho. With this, the north fell for the first time to a power grouping outside the central tradition. Occasionally, nomadic or semi-nomadic tribes had encroached on the verges of this region. But now dozens of alien rulers were to hold sway in the traditional nucleus of China for a length of time that ran into centuries.

The foreign rule of north China between 317 and 589 has often been compared with the roughly contemporary invasion of the Roman empire by Germanic tribes. There are in fact parallels, but as so often with comparable historical cases, the differences are more enlightening than the likenesses. The two nuclei, in the Greek east and the Latin west, were enough on their own to ensure that the Roman empire had always been more heterogeneous than the north and south of China. By contrast there remained in China, even when divided, close cultural and personal contacts between the heartland of Chinese civilization in the north, which continued to be the most densely populated part, and the regions in the south that gradually filled with refugees. Chinese remained not only the *lingua franca* serving practical needs, but also the only literary medium, for historians as well as all other writers, in both parts of the country. True, governmental organization in the 'barbarian' north and the Chinese south evolved in ways that in some respects differed considerably. Special cultural forms developed too, but these were offset by mutual borrowings. The alien cult of Buddhism for instance, spread more easily in the north to begin with, but then soon gained adherents among the princely class in the traditionally conservative south. It is hardly possible to speak of genuine isolation of the two regions. The northern and southern halves of China were separated by no geographical boundaries worthy of the name, nor by any insuperable ethnic barriers. In spite of two and a half centuries of foreign domination in the north, China remained to a very large extent an integrated cultural entity. The exact numerical ratio of the foreign rulers and the people they conquered is not known. But it was so disproportionate that to stay in power, the foreigners, who had overrun north China at a moment of weakness and division, in a few lightning campaigns, were soon forced to share at least some of their power with the traditional forces of law and order, the large landowners who had remained *in situ*. Many invaders went over to the Chinese life style with the passage of time, and intermarried with the Chinese substratum; culturally they became Chinese themselves. When, towards the end of the sixth century, the child of a mixed marriage, the later Sui Emperor Wen-ti (reigned 589–605), first seized the throne of the state of Chou from his non-Chinese father-in-law and then proceeded with the conquest of the south, where the concept of the unified state had remained in force without interruption, he met with hardly any opposition worth mention. This was partly due to his military superiority, but also partly to the fact that he was acknowledged as culturally Chinese. Later authors claimed that the transforming strength of Chinese civilization had asserted itself, just as it had in the Chou period when there had again been no convincing central ruler capable of uniting the realm. This transcending power was upheld by thoroughly solid facts: the numerical superiority of the Chinese, and the particular way in which their agrarian society was organized. These two factors, above all others, ensured the survival of the essential Chinese identity throughout long periods of foreign domination. They played their part in later periods when Chinese territory was subdued by culturally alien minorities, such as the Kitan-Liao, the Jurchen-Chin, the Mongol-Yüan and the Manchu-Ch'ing. Where the rest of the world was concerned the concept of transforming strength and the ideology of superior civilization proved ineffectual. The two concrete foundations did not stretch as far as the world outside, which was to be won only by military force or commercial attractions. In other words, there was a qualitative difference in China's 'powers of persuasion' inside and outside the frontiers of her civilization.

The Chinese conception of themselves as a civilization and a state – more precisely, their image of the position in the world of the Son of Heaven and his realm, which had been little more than an ideal in the later Chou period – could be regarded as fully realized under the T'ang. The idea of a united empire had been confirmed in fact, and the empire was co-terminous with the extent of Chinese civilization. If the paramountcy of the Ch'in and the Han had seemed an exceptional case in an essentially polycentric structure, the rule of the Sui and the succeeding T'ang was undisputably a confirmation of the principle of unity. The Chinese opinion of themselves and the outside world moved into a new phase after the experience of rule by foreigners, although many features seemed merely to confirm what was already known. History appeared to be simply repeating itself, even in details. The Ch'in-Han and Sui-T'ang relationship as, respectively, forerunner and 'major' dynasty, has already been mentioned. Li Yüan (566–635) and

Li Shih-min (reigned as T'ang T'ai-tsung 626–49), the founders of the T'ang dynasty, also had the help of foreign tribes in seizing the throne; and these allies too later turned against them (624). On this occasion, however, the dynasty was strong enough to expel the foreigners (630).

Although thus confirmed in its concept of itself, the T'ang empire was not isolationist in its early days. The multitudinous regional peculiarities evolved during the years of division were to begin with adopted by the empire, along with traditional structures, without any noteworthy dilution. A receptive attitude towards the outside world and a sense of China's superiority were not mutually exclusive. Buddhism, the most important cultural import of the first millennium AD, was able to extend. It had gained a foothold in nearly all the separate states during the time of division, but had been especially successful in the north. The new range of ideas had a most profound effect in China, not only on religion, but on philosophy and the language as well. The study of the sacred texts, which were mostly in Sanskrit, led to a better understanding of the students' own idiom. The thoughts expressed in the foreign language enhanced conceptual thought and logic, but above all they immeasurably enriched art and literature. In Buddhism, the Chinese encountered for the first time pure metaphysics and a transcendental doctrine of salvation. A whole series of other foreign religions also enjoyed imperial patronage under the early T'ang. Mazdaism, the teaching of Zoroaster, had already reached China during the sixth century. During the eighth century the T'ang realm contained Nestorians, Manichaeans, Jews and Moslems. Though the majority of them were foreigners, some were temporary residents, such as ambassadors and trade delegates; but many more were permanent, such as mercenaries, actors, merchants and monks. The numbers of these foreign residents ran into tens or possibly even hundreds of thousands, for China's trade links with the rest of the world were greater at that time than ever before, and the majority of that trade, on both the continental and the maritime frontiers, was carried on by foreigners. The capital, Ch'ang-an, lay at the end of the Silk Road, the central Asia trade route, and was itself one of the great centres of foreign trade. A busy trade with the Near East and India grew up in Canton, which established itself as the major port in the south at this period. There were sizeable Arab communities in Canton and some of the other larger ports, who lived in enclaves, under their own laws. So far as is known they created the precedent for the legally instituted extraterritoriality which was extended later to Europeans, such as the

Portuguese in Macao from 1557 onwards, and for the concessions granted in a number of towns in the nineteenth century. The foreigners and their property were not subject to Chinese authority, but had their own administration and judicial systems. This concession did not imply any ceding of Chinese territory, and was not regarded primarily as a concession at all by the Chinese. The concentration of the foreigners in quarters that bore some resemblance to ghettoes was desirable from the point of view of public order and considerably simplified administration.

The early T'ang empire's sense of its strength and superiority gave it the confidence to open its doors freely to the world outside. For the same reason, however, the numerous influences from outside, with a few exceptions such as Buddhism and the precedents for the role of foreigners in trade, made little enduring impression. The structure of Chinese society and political institutions, for instance, were virtually untouched by foreign influences. China was the model and the source of civilization, and the Chinese knew all there was to know about it. A number of states formed round the periphery of the Chinese empire during the T'ang era, from societies hitherto with little or no form of advanced political organization. All of them modelled themselves on the Chinese example: 'Tibet' (607), 'Japan' (645), Silla [Korea] (668), P'o-hai [south-east Manchuria] (713) and Nan-chao [Yünnan] (740). China's relationship with the outside world rapidly changed in the second half of the T'ang period. The Chinese defeat by an Arab army at the battle of Talas (Ferghana) in 751 was merely the incident that incited exclusion of the outside world and everything alien. The decisive motives were internal: financial, political and ideological. Reference has already been made to the substantial privileges Buddhist monasteries had secured for themselves, enabling accumulation of great wealth exempt from state taxation. When the state fell into financial difficulties, the Buddhist institutions came into the front line of criticism. The most loudly voiced strictures were admittedly always philosophical and moral, such as the accusations made by Confucians, that is, by the civil service, that the celibacy enjoined by Buddhism was an offence to people's duty to their ancestors. In spite of enjoying the patronage of rulers in the southern states since the fifth century, Buddhism never lost the stigma of being a foreign religion, especially in Confucian eyes. The fact that Buddhism itself changed, doctrinally and institutionally, to adapt to the spiritual, intellectual and social circumstances of China, made no difference. Orthodox Confucians regarded themselves as the sole guardians of the Chinese tradition and jealously strove to prevent the emperor taking any other view. To them Buddhism was the cultural appendage of the military invasion by foreign races. The years 841 to 845 saw the most thoroughgoing campaign of secularization that was ever directed against Buddhism. Its principal targets were the Buddhist church, the bonzes and the priests, rather than individual laymen. Buddhism as an organization did not recover from this blow. No more did the institutions of other alien religions which were attacked and dissolved during the same period, less on account of their material possessions than of their foreignness. The weakening of the central government and the decline of the internal order of the state led Chinese society to withdraw into itself and soon brought on a fundamental aversion against all things foreign. A massacre in Canton by Huang Ch'ao's rebels is supposed to have cost the lives of over 100,000 foreigners, mostly Moslems (879). This incident was only a particularly blatant expression of the xenophobia that was flaring up in China. With the resumption and tightening of the Confucian state examination system, educated Chinese, too, withdrew their interest from alien traditions, especially Buddhism. The reversion to the native tradition closed the doors that had been open under the early T'ang. The consequence of growing internal insecurity was a hardening of attitudes towards the outside world and foreign influences.

Internal stability was restored by the early Sung emperors but they were left with relatively little external influence. In the interim, states on the Chinese model had established themselves around the empire, or were in the process of doing so, and were not easily to be pushed aside. But in all probability it was not only the situation on the frontiers that had changed, but also the mood of internal politics. Military commanders, who had still had a decisive influence on events under the T'ang, were now less highly regarded than civilian administrators. The destructive effect of military intervention in internal affairs had produced a reaction under the Sung in favour of civilian procedures. One result was that the expansionist policies usually pursued by major dynasties in the past gave way to an essentially defensive posture. Indeed, from this time forth, with perhaps a single exception, the Ming Emperor Ch'eng-tsu (reigned 1403–25), the only genuinely expansionist campaigns were carried out by foreign rulers, principally the Mongols and the Manchu. This restriction of strategic activity to the existing frontiers was paralleled, as had already been foreshadowed

145

in the second half of the T'ang period, by a concentration on specifically Chinese values and exclusion of all influences from the outside world. The treaties that the Sung made with the strongest of their neighbours shed a particularly interesting light on the way China's relations with the rest of the world developed. Once the parties involved had recognized that they could not overcome their opponents, the agreements served to institutionalize a coexistence that differed considerably from previous military stalemates. In the year 1005 the Sung Emperor Chen-tsung (reigned 998–1023) and the ruler of the Liao-Kitan concluded a treaty at Shan-yüan, including the clause that each acknowledged the other's right to the title of emperor. That a ruling Chinese emperor should recognize a foreigner as an emperor (*huang-ti*) in the central tradition was unheard of. The situation was a fundamental contradiction of the traditional theory, that there could not be two suns in the heavens, nor two Sons of Heaven on earth. The fact that the Sung emperor was acknowledged as the 'elder brother' of the Liao emperor was neither here nor there. Not surprisingly, the Treaty of Shan-yüan was the subject of violent controversy during the Sung period, and continued to be criticized by orthodox historians of later periods. Compared with this concession on a point of principle and the shameful surrender it represented to dogmatic Confucians, other clauses, in which the Sung agreed to pay the Liao annual 'compensation', i.e. tribute, went almost unnoticed, although the sum involved amounted on average to 2 per cent of the budget. The Treaty of Shan-yüan was not unique: the Sung emperors' policy of coexistence, however painful the rupture with traditional ideology, is further illustrated by their agreements with the contiguous Tangut-Tibetan state of Hsi-Hsia, based in the farther Ordos region, which it was also militarily impossible to dislodge. In 1043 Sung Jen-tsung (reigned 1023–64) acknowledged the imperial title (*huang-ti*) of the ruler of Hsi-Hsia. Once again the fabrication of a familial hierarchy – the emperor of Hsi-Hsia became the 'son' of the Sung emperor – conserved the fiction of a difference in rank. Naturally, annual 'compensation' was paid to Hsi-Hsia too.

This delicately balanced triangular relationship dominated the Sung period, even after the Chin-Jurchen had knocked the Liao-Kitan out of the ring in the early twelfth century and forced the Sung to withdraw to the Huaiho line. Opinion is divided as to the efficacy of this policy, but there is no denying that it preserved the *status quo* for nearly a century without any great strain on military resources. The Chin

146

invasion cannot be regarded as a direct consequence of this policy. Rather it arose from a renewed attempt of the 'Militant' party, which pushed its way to the fore at the beginning of the twelfth century, spurred on by the eunuch T'ung Kuan (d. 1126), to 'restrain the barbarians by playing off one against the other' (*i-i chih-i*). This method, a traditional ploy of Chinese foreign policy, was always controversial, and continued to be so until the twentieth century. It was especially so when the Chinese overestimated their own strength, as in the early twelfth century. T'ung Kuan saw his chance when the Jurchen rose against the Kitan in 1114 and came to an agreement with them in 1115. When the two parties finally combined in open war against Liao-Kitan in 1122–23 the Jurchen bore the main brunt of it. Both considered themselves cheated over the division of the enemy's territory. The Sung, however, were too weak to press their own interests, while the Chin-Jurchen took not only their great ally's share of the spoils but also a sizeable piece of his territory. It was not until 1142–43 that Chancellor Ch'in Kuei (1090–1155) and his 'Pacific' party, representing principally the great southern landowners, succeeded in negotiating peace terms. The Sung were obliged not only to pay substantial 'compensation' but also formally to recognize the Huai-Wei line as the frontier and even declare themselves the vassals of the Chin. It was undoubtedly the greatest humiliation a Chinese ruler had ever experienced up to that date. Understandably the appeasers, especially Ch'in Kuei himself, went down in history as betrayers of the empire and of the whole proper order of things. In fact, the Sung repeated their error, when they encouraged the Mongols to destroy the Chin. The Mongols annihilated the Chin in 1234, without the Sung gaining any advantage from it at all. Quite the reverse: it opened the way for the Mongols to overrun what was left of the Sung empire.

With the move of the political and economic centre of gravity in the south to the coast – Lin-an (Hangchou) became the Sung capital in 1138 – and with the traditional trade contacts with central Asia barred by a powerful enemy state to the north, the Southern Sung had to reorientate their foreign policy and more particularly their foreign economic relations. The sea and the coast became the principal arenas for trading, and maritime contacts became the principal links with the outside world. For the first time the full political and strategic relevance of the maritime frontier was recognized, and control was systematically extended over the waters parallel to the coastline. Now that the capital lay so close to the coast it was recognized that the sea no longer constituted an automatic defence. Seaborne flanking attacks by the Chin were the prime fear. From the Southern Sung onwards China ceased to be exclusively a continental state and became to a certain extent a seafaring nation. This development was paralleled in her society. Chinese merchants and sailors took the place of the foreigners who had dominated that sphere under the T'ang. In the twelfth century the great majority of seaborne trade and traffic as far as Japan and the islands of south-east Asia was in Chinese hands. The state took direct control of maritime trading by establishing Shipping Authorities (*shih-po-ssu*) invested with the sole right to transact overseas business. Shipping authorities had already existed under the T'ang, but this was the first time that the state had established a monopoly over ocean sailing, that is, over all maritime traffic. The system of state supervision and the limiting of trade to a few places, which led to serious confrontations with the European powers in the nineteenth century, was developed in full under the Sung.

During the years when the Sung ruled in the south, the territory which had been settled by the Chinese was broken up into three distinct polities. The states of Chin and Hsi-Hsia both included considerable areas of semi-desert and forested steppe to the north, as well as the fundamentally different terrain of the original Chinese heartland. But, as under earlier foreign dominion, Chinese society remained virtually unchanged in the long run, either in its structure or in its concept of itself. It was above all this quality of invariability that defined China as a historical continuum. There had of course always been a 'legitimate' Han-Chinese dynasty in control somewhere or other in the country during the intervals of foreign rule. In that respect the Mongol conquest of the whole of China was a fundamental change. The Mongol khans were the first foreigners to hold sole sway over the realm of the Son of Heaven. When Chinese historians and political theorists admitted after the end of Mongol rule that the mandate of heaven had undoubtedly fallen to foreigners, it was true, at least in so far as no successful rival candidate had come forward as an indisputable sign from heaven. Until the area occupied and previously governed by Chinese had been conquered in full, the assumption that the mandate of heaven was a prerogative of the Han Chinese, on account of their cultural superiority, had never seriously been questioned. Although the Mongol success was plainly the result of overwhelming strength, with no cultural pretensions to it, the historians had to designate the Mongol emperors legitimate, or else imply a complete disruption of

148

legitimate government in the world. It is significant, however, that the official histories, at least, which were so important in defining the national identity, on the whole avoided explaining the nature of the Mongol tenure of the Celestial Throne. A few centuries later, when the throne had been seized by the Manchu, the scholar Ku Yen-wu (1613–82) came up with the formula that a dynasty (*kuo-chia*) might fall, but the empire itself (*t'ien-hsia*) would not, so long as the Chinese remained Chinese and did not become barbarians and surrender the specific qualities of their humanity (*jen-tao*). Modern Chinese writers have adhered to this construction (Ch'ien Mu).

The conqueror of the Sung, Kublai Khan (1215–94), like nearly all the foreign rulers in China before him, had assimilated himself to the Chinese imperial tradition. He did not overthrow the Celestial Throne but mounted it himself (1280), after he had formally founded a new dynasty, the Yüan, in the traditional Chinese manner (1260). He bestowed a posthumous Chinese title on his grandfather Jenghis Khan (*c.* 1155–1227), and he tried to justify his policies by the Confucian principles of government legitimized by heaven. All the same, the Mongol government was largely an exception in the overall pattern of Chinese history. Its relations with the outside world were not the least influence setting it apart. The Yüan state was only one part of a giant Mongol dominion, reaching via the fraternal khanates of Chagatai (Turkestan) and Kipchak (southern and central Russia), and the ilkhanate of Iran (Persia), as far as Europe and the Near East. It was during this period that the first historically authenticated journeys of Europeans in Asia were made: by merchants such as Maffio, Niccolo and Marco Polo (in China 1262–66 and 1275–92) and papal legates such as Montecorvino (in China 1295–1332; Archbishop of Khanbalik-Peking from 1307), Pordenone (in China 1324–28) and Marignolli (in China 1342–47). On the Pacific side, large armadas sailed as far as Japan (1274, 1281) and Java (1281–92); in south-east Asia armies on land invaded Annam (1286) and Burma (1278, 1283). Ambassadors travelled to demand submission from states in India, Ceylon, Taiwan and the Indo-Chinese archipelago. This energetic policy of expansion was condemned by a critic in the Ch'ing period as the first attempts to extend the territory of the empire overseas 'by stealth'. It was certainly new for China, in the name of the Son of Heaven, to take an overseas initiative, displaying force to win sovereignty or diplomatic contacts in areas where she had not previously ventured. It is debatable whether these forays differed fundamentally in motivation from those made by

149

the Han and T'ang emperors into south-east Asia. The Mongols had the technical and personal support of Chinese in these adventures. If China's doors were open to the world under the early T'ang, under the Yüan she was linked to the whole of Eurasia. The first 'authentic' maps of the world were drawn under the Mongol empire, in which not only Asia and Europe but Africa too are depicted, broadly speaking with accuracy (*Yü-t'u* by Chu Ssu-pen [1273–1337]; *Sheng-chiao kuang-pei t'u* by Li Tse-min [*fl.* 1330]).

The worldwide contacts and enlarged world view of the Yüan period made only a superficial impression on the Chinese, however, especially the educated classes in the south. Although they are recorded in the official and semi-official histories, they did not greatly change the national consciousness. Particularly just after the departure of the Mongol emperors, the Chinese saw no reason to accept the idea of a polycentric world in which other nations were equal to their own. On the contrary: the Mongols had contributed to the conviction of Chinese superiority and to the antipathy towards foreigners which had grown, as probably never before, to be the correlative of the Chinese sense of cultural and ethnic identity. Unlike alien rulers of other periods, the Mongols had kept themselves apart from the Chinese, as a distinct, isolated governing race. One reason for that may well have been that the Mongols were nomads through and through, and remained so essentially, not least because of their close and abiding contacts with their central Asian homeland. Certainly they kept their cultural individuality longer than other foreign rulers. The bitter struggle to conquer the south, dragging on for decades; the discrimination against former subjects of the Southern Sung; the employment and preferment of foreign mercenaries and administrators who were sometimes more alien to China than the Mongols themselves; the political isolation of the traditionally privileged classes, especially in the south; the toleration and encouragement of old, discarded religions (Taoism, Buddhism) and of new, alien ones (Islam, Christianity) at the expense of Confucianism, which had regained its pre-eminence from the mid-T'ang onwards: all these had moved the southern Chinese of every social class to pronounced hostility towards foreigners, which had hardened into racism and xenophobia. The development was paralleled by a stronger and almost exclusive preoccupation with Chinese values and the Chinese tradition. The outcome of this process has sometimes been called Chinese nationalism by commentators. However, while it undoubtedly bears certain resemblances to European

150

forms of nationalism, the most interesting thing about it, once again, is the points at which it diverges from the European pattern. This is especially so with the identification of the political and the cultural entity, of the state and the civilization. Every crack that appeared in the smooth surface quickly vanished again. Time, the incontestable survival of the 'central' tradition, could not help but appear to the Chinese as the 'tracer element of reality' (Heuss). As long as there was a Chinese culture, that is, as long as there were Chinese people, China could not disappear from the face of the earth. China could not be absorbed into some other entity; the most another entity could do was take China by force. The Chinese tradition was central, and the tradition survived. The overthrow of the Mongol rulers was a renewed confirmation of that. Postulated nearly two thousand years before the Ming as a Utopian ideal that had existed at an even earlier date, the superiority of the central tradition had step by step, in the alternation of unity and division, of Chinese and non-Chinese domination, proved its reality. The representatives of the tradition could see no contradiction between the claim and the reality. The extent to which the ideal of world order transmitted in the Confucian canon was regarded as realized under the Ming is illustrated by the fact that the ideal was understood by then to have been exemplified in the T'ang period as well, and not in the distant past alone. It was therefore only logical that the founder of the Ming exhorted his successors to 'rule like the T'ang'.

There is one other question with regard to the Mongol regime that must be mentioned. Ossip K. Flechtheim has expressed the view that the Mongols in Russia prevented the transition from a natural, agrarian economy to the commercial and industrial capitalist economy that was going on in Europe in the same period. The question has particular relevance to China in view of the fact that under the Sung emperors, immediately prior to the Yüan, China had experienced an unprecedented forward surge in the evolution of her urban culture, of manufacture, commerce and communications. If these incipient capitalist developments did not lead to the same results in China as in western Europe, it can hardly be blamed on the Mongols. So far as is known, they did nothing to reverse the course of economic development. The decisive factors are more likely to have been the absolutism of the Ming and the conservatism of the Ch'ing.

From the first the Ming empire was a closed-door state, hermetically sealed against the outside world. Foreign contacts were the privilege of the state and could be made only under licence. On several occasions the first Ming emperor, T'ai-tsu (reigned 1368–98), issued strict regulations governing the crossing of frontiers and the good conduct of foreigners inside China. An elaborate system of frontier defences, including the coastline, was built up. While there was nothing new in the principle of all this, the intensity and rigour of the practice were without precedent. But the policy was not simply an expression of exaggerated sino-centricity. It was a strategic necessity, for the frontier areas in central Asia, along the coast and in the western provinces, had become the refuge of the dynastic rivals and opponents of the Ming, both Chinese and alien. The western provinces of Yünnan and Ssechuan were conquered and added to the empire in 1382. But in spite of occasional forays and numerous defensive measures the continental and maritime frontiers were at risk throughout the whole period. Perhaps surprisingly, in view of the military power with which the dynasty was established, the Ming state must be looked upon as weak. Militarily, with a few exceptions, it remained purely on the defensive. It attempted, and accomplished, hardly any territorial additions; it did not bring the remoter corners of the T'ang empire under its direct control. Nowhere was the Ming frontier bordered by an area unoccupied by another power. Consequently the political and geographic integrity of the empire had to be defended and safeguarded at great effort and expense. More even than under the Sung, China was thrown in upon herself, territorially as well as in other respects. In the sphere of diplomacy and politics the Ming were less defensive than in matters of strategy. On the contrary, particularly in the early years of the regime, confidence in the greatness of their state led them to take the initiative, even to show occasional aggression. The dynamic impetus began to slacken in the middle of the fifteenth century, but the institutional framework of external relations survived. That applied above all to the tribute system, which was the correlative of the military safeguards. The tribute system was the clearest manifestation of China's attitude to the outside world and of her concept of her own relative position. As already indicated, it was not invented by the Ming, but it was developed by them in a form that the Ch'ing, too, found completely acceptable. Eventually it was the cause, or pretext, for the confrontations between the imperial government and the western powers several centuries later. This was particularly so in its ritual trappings – emissaries had to kneel three times before the emperor and touch the floor with their heads nine times (k'ou-t'ou: kotow).

152

Immediately after founding the Ming dynasty, Emperor T'ai-tsu sent emissaries to several near-by countries to announce his accession. This kind of use of diplomatic missions became the regular practice, especially when there was a change of emperor. The Ming emperors always deported themselves as the chosen Sons of Heaven, of course, but the impression remains that they needed the recognition of the outside world, perhaps not least in order to support their claims to internal authority. Soon after T'ai-tsu's accession the first ambassadors arrived to felicitate the new ruler in China, and thereby to acknowledge him as the ruler *of* China. Naturally everything was performed with the politeness and show of respect customary at that time and in that country; naturally the ambassadors were also the bearers of gifts. Their trouble and their expense were rewarded with gifts from the emperor in return, and at the same time the countries they represented entered the 'inner circle' enjoying a special relationship with China (*wu-wai*), instead of remaining in the darkness outside the circle (*wai*). This system whereby foreign princes recognized the emperor of China, and the emperor affirmed them on their thrones in return was the chief manifestation of the non-military relationships between the Ming state and the outside world. The accompanying exchange of gifts often took on the character of a genuine trading exchange. But it remained in theory, especially in Chinese eyes, an integral part of the political action.

Before the diplomatic initiatives inaugurated by T'ai-tsu settled down into a steady routine, they were surpassed by the third Ming emperor, Ch'eng-tsu (reigned 1403–25). No fewer than forty-eight delegations were dispatched in his name, to visit countries in the vicinity of China and farther afield. He sent seven immense fleets, under the command of eunuchs, out across the southern and western oceans, to the Indo-Chinese archipelago, India, the Persian Gulf and the Red Sea. Some of the ships reached the east coast of Africa. The size of the fleets alone (62 ships and 28,000 men in 1405–7) shows clearly that the emperor's intention was to make an unambiguous show of force and in this they succeeded. The court clocked up several dozen new tributaries, who were also, by definition, vassals. Embassies came to China from Hormuz on the Persian Gulf and from Africa four times, from Bengal eleven times and from Malacca four times. But the ambassadors did not always travel of their own free will: the princes of Palembang (Sumatra) and Ceylon, for instance, were carried off to Nanking by force. It is transparently clear that nothing short of the

153

naked display of his strength could have moved the 'barbarians' to pay tribute to an emperor in faraway China. The pressed delegations soon ceased when Ch'eng-tsu's successors put a stop to the costly fleets in 1433. A lot of reasons have been put forward for the end of this aggressive, seaborne diplomacy: the latent antagonism between officials and eunuchs, the prohibitive financial outlay, the renewed menace on the northern land frontier, the absence of a commercial lobby and the introversion and complacency of the influential upper class. They all doubtless played some part, but there was another, personal factor. Self-assertion and formal recognition mattered less to the successor Ming emperors than they did to Ch'eng-tsu. Unlike him, the usurper, hardly any of them were required to prove their right to the throne. The cessation of the maritime enterprises had, it now appears, far-reaching consequences. Only a matter of decades after the Ming had withdrawn their presence from the seas between China and Africa, European navigators penetrated them, and gradually established a relay of landfalls and settlements. From these they soon made their first advances to China, and eventually they served as the bases for military attacks on the empire in the nineteenth century.

Unlike the European states in what was for them the age of exploration and discovery, there was next to no governmental interest in foreign trade in China. The Ming emperors and their civil service alike were opposed to commerce, an attitude hallowed by ideological tradition. But the ideology had a footing in sound realism. By its very nature, trade is movement, and as such threatens the stability of every system which is concerned with preserving the *status quo*. This is true, above all, of trade across frontiers, which adds the element of ambivalent loyalties to the dangers of mobility. It is not uncommon for the population of frontier areas to have better relations with the countries across the borders than with their own government. Another of the advantages of foreign trade is the greater likelihood of profit, due to the different levels of exchange rates. To guard against the twin dangers of mobility and ambivalent loyalty, the first Ming emperor introduced strict regulations which reduced commercial traffic across the frontiers of the empire to an absolute minimum. The Southern Sung had set up the Shipping Authorities at the time when maritime commerce was flourishing but their prime purpose had been to collect tax on the trade. Under the Ming, and under the Ch'ing too, the same institution, the Shipping Authorities, exercised what were first and foremost strategical and political controls. They were the channels through which the embassies bringing tribute from abroad entered the empire. These delegations were restricted in frequency and size. They were the only officially approved instruments of foreign trade, and functioned in two ways: in the exchange of tribute from them and gifts from the emperor, which officially did not count as trade, and in the licence given to merchants who accompanied the missions to sell certain goods on a free market, which was classified as 'supplementary tribute'. The official Chinese attitude to this trade was that it was a favour, compensating for the dangers of the journey and satisfying the 'foolish striving of foreigners for profit'. In fact, China benefited from the trade, too, and not only financially. It was the means whereby she obtained important raw materials. Japanese missions, for instance, frequently imported several thousand tons of copper and sulphur. This method of paying tribute was supposed to be the only form of foreign trade. The Ming attitude to the trade was that it was an unimportant adjunct to the political act of submission on the part of the foreigners, and an act of indulgence towards them. The foreigners, on the other hand, frequently regarded it as the most important part of their dealings as China's tributaries. They did everything they could to increase the frequency and scale of the exchanges, either by arriving in China at times other than those laid down for them, or by claiming to bear tribute from non-existent potentates, or simply by ignoring the prescribed limitations on the amounts of goods they were allowed to carry. A delegation arrived in 1618, for instance, purporting to come from the kingdom of Rum (i.e. the eastern Roman empire); the Mongol Oirat sent several thousand men to China almost every year from 1408 onwards, to collect thousands of bales of silk in exchange for their relatively modest 'tribute'. Some nations won other trade concessions, such as the special frontier markets that the Mongol Tümet were allowed to set up in the mid-sixteenth century. None of these actions and concessions can seriously be regarded as anything but gestures of appeasement on the part of the Chinese. The tribute system, apart from its ideological and diplomatic function, had been intended first and foremost as an instrument of control. It proved powerless, in fact, to prevent the growth of intensive private, that is, illegal, trading. On the contrary, it was encouraged by the very exclusivity of the system. Since this private foreign trading took place outside the law, the unrest of the frontier regions was aggravated by smuggling and piracy. The activity of the so-called 'Japanese pirates' (*wo-k'ou*), most of whom were in fact Chinese, and who plagued the

Chinese coasts for several decades in the sixteenth century, is a very typical example. The connection between piracy and the outlawing of trade was clear enough to some contemporaries, such as the government official T'ang Shu (1497–1574): 'Pirates and merchants are identical with each other. If trade is allowed, the pirates will become merchants. If trade is forbidden, the merchants will become pirates.' To most Chinese officials however, the connection was merely additional proof of the reprehensibility of trade. This conclusion proved prejudicial, too, to the Portuguese who made the first official landfall in a Chinese port in 1517. They made things worse for themselves by their 'barbarian' behaviour and customs, such as firing a salute as they sailed in, and they were soon told to leave. It was not until 1557 that the Portuguese, like the Arabs of the T'ang period, were granted an enclave, which eventually became Macao. Also in the middle of the sixteenth century, Chinese merchants, too, after long and stubborn representations, won the right to a modest degree of trading outside the limits of the tribute system. The system, however, continued to operate.

The European expeditions to China brought with them a group of people who were not interested in commerce, and not to be discouraged in their persistent efforts to penetrate the empire's locked doors: Christian missionaries. In 1583 the first entry permit since the Mongol emperors was granted to two missionaries, one of whom was the Jesuit Matteo Ricci (1552–1610). Ricci's success in China was not an accident. He showed exceptional insight, amenability and respect for the Chinese character and culture in his efforts to establish a base for his mission in China. An at early stage he realized that he would do best to begin with the educated governing class. Accordingly he studied their customs and manners as well as the Confucian texts and tried to conform with them in his own behaviour. This was of course exactly what Confucian theory expected of a 'barbarian', when he came into contact with Chinese civilization. As Ricci persevered in his studies, or, as it seemed to the Chinese, as he was assimilated to their ways (lai-hua), he had the opportunity to expound his beliefs and his learning to the scholars with whom he came into contact. Influential recommendations gained him permission to go to Peking; the emperor received him in audience. The source of Ricci's unusual success lay primarily in his own personality. But it also illustrates that even in the xenophobic Ming empire individuals within the governing class were interested in intellectual contacts with foreigners, providing the latter showed tact

156

and were cultured in the Chinese sense. During the latter part of the Ming regime and still under the first two Ch'ing emperors, the Jesuits successfully consolidated their position in China. There can be no doubt, however, that the fathers owed their rise in Chinese esteem to the eminently practical assistance they rendered the governments of both dynasties. It was above all in the fields of mathematics, astronomy and weapon technology that they proved most useful; the court entrusted them with the reform of the calendar, and they prepared specifications for the construction of improved cannon. In 1645 the Jesuit Johann Adam Schall von Bell (1591–1666), a native of Cologne, was appointed director of the Astronomical Office, a senior post in the civil service. This appointment, integrating a foreigner in the existing official and social hierarchy, did more than enhance his position and influence. In so far as it made him directly responsible to the Chinese authorities, it also made it possible to render acceptable, in Chinese eyes, those foreigners whom the state either needed, or (as in the case of the European commissioners of the Maritime Customs Service in the nineteenth century) was forced to employ. This process created fewer problems for a foreign dynasty like the Manchu-Ch'ing, or the Mongol-Yüan before them, than for a Chinese dynasty. The former in any case usually had to rely on specialists of different races from themselves. The Jesuits' original purpose was to convert the emperor and, following him, the whole empire, on the analogy of Constantine and the Romans. They never came anywhere near their goal. The teaching of Christian doctrine was banned by the second Ch'ing emperor. Even so, it had been the first time for centuries that some sections, at least, of the upper classes had come into contact with an intellectual and spiritual world comparable in stature to their own tradition.

The contacts did not achieve any fundamental alteration in the Chinese concept of themselves or in their relations with the rest of the world, even after the Manchu ascended the Celestial Throne. This was because, unlike the Mongols, who had mainly sought to legitimize their seizure of power merely by formal adoption of Chinese traditions, the Manchu were more thorough in their attempts to 'equal the T'ang'. Consequently, under the alien dynasty from the north, traditional China experienced its last great flowering. The foreign emperors and their Chinese administrators re-created, and maintained for over a century, a state of affairs almost ideal from the viewpoint of traditional concepts. Up to about 1800 the empire enjoyed an internal peace and

157

stability such as Europe had seldom known for so long a period. Undertakings in foreign affairs were successful and earned respect and deference for the emperor and his realm; the economy prospered; the arts and scholarship flourished. The Manchu purpose was not to change but to strengthen the traditional order of things; their success was ample proof that Heaven had bestowed its mandate upon them. The traditional Chinese concepts of order in society and in the universe, the organization and administration of the state that had been built up over so many centuries, were not only not tampered with under the Ch'ing, they were dogmatically reinforced. It can be seen in retrospect that this very stability and preservation of what was considered an ideal tradition were the reasons for the rapidity of decline in the nineteenth century. The state and the society were quite exceptionally incapable of adapting themselves to changed conditions. But even this incapacity was not of Ch'ing origin, but inherent in the traditional structure and attitudes.

When considering China's foreign relations under the Ch'ing emperors, the distinction must again be made between inner and outer circles, between Chinese-Manchu relations and the relations of the Ch'ing empire with the rest of the world. The Chinese continued to regard the Manchu as foreigners, their earnest and successful endeavours on behalf of the Chinese tradition notwithstanding. The dominant Manchu minority, like other alien rulers before them, felt an obligation to preserve their identity. They instituted a series of regulations and measures designed to protect it, such as forbidding Chinese to enter Manchuria, making the study of their native language compulsory for all Manchu, and forbidding the Manchu to engage in trade or labour, or to intermarry with Chinese. The broad mass of the Chinese population were in no way worse off than they had been under the Chinese Ming, but they could hardly fail to be aware of the privileges and isolation of the Manchu. It was on this awareness that the salvationist ideologies of the nineteenth-century secret societies were able to work and convert into rebellion. The relationship of the educated and wealthy classes with the foreign rulers was more delicately balanced. After it had become clear that the Manchu, unlike the Mongols, had no intention of upsetting the existing social hierarchy, but wanted the support of educated Chinese, only convinced Ming loyalists withheld their cooperation. In fact there were still quite a large number of the latter in the seventeenth century, many of them among the greatest thinkers of the age, such as Huang Tsung-hsi

(1610–95), Wang Fu-chih (1619–92) and Ku Yen-wu (1613–82). By the eighteenth century antagonism between the ruling Manchu and the Chinese upper class was the exception rather than the rule.

As so often in the past, the foreigners had been invited into China by a Chinese border commander. Wu San-kuei (1612–78) had sought their help, in 1644, to crush a rebel, Li Tzu-ch'eng (c. 1605–45), who was in possession of Peking at the time. Although Wu San-kuei assisted the Manchu to establish their dynasty in Peking, his real intention was to seize power for himself eventually. He rose against the Ch'ing in 1673, but no more successfully than many others who had entertained similar hopes of using 'barbarians' to further their own dynastic ambitions. It had always proved a particularly dangerous ploy when China was weak and the 'barbarians' were asked to help, not beyond the frontiers, but inside the Great Wall itself. The Manchu had intervened in China's internal disputes and justified their seizure of power by that very act. They presented themselves, not as aggressors, but as the only party who had been capable of restoring peace and civil order by suppressing the rebels who had overthrown the Ming. All the institutions left behind by the Ming, many of which the Manchu already emulated in their own country, remained intact. Nothing was changed in the social structure, including the privileges and duties bound up in it. The Manchu safeguarded their position by setting up a centralized military organization, consisting mainly of Manchu troops – Chinese units served only as scattered 'police' forces – and by duplicating all the senior posts in the civil service.

The relationship of the Chinese and the Manchu has often been discussed. One reason is that the abundance of original sources enables unusually detailed study of the governmental practices of a foreign dynasty. Another reason is that it is assumed to be particularly illuminating about China's relations with her immediate neighbours. There is relative agreement on the separate stages of how these relations developed; but not how a small foreign minority might at all control so large and complex a society as China. One point of view is that a rigorous minority, just large enough to sustain a dynasty, fill the top posts in the administration and man the key military contingents, would probably always be capable of imposing itself on a largely compartmented society like that of traditional China. Another view is that the Manchu could only maintain their power by the same means as earlier alien dynasties of the second millennium, that is, by adapting themselves to the central Chinese tradition. Indeed it is maintained that they were already so far assimilated into Chinese civilization by the time they seized power that it is hardly appropriate to describe them as alien at all. There is some truth in both these views, but two other interrelated factors should also be adduced: the high degree of centralization in the power structure and the readiness of the wealthy and educated upper class to cooperate in the administration of power with practically any master who was both strong enough to hold them in check, and willing to guarantee them their privileges. The last two factors enabled them more than anything else to move into control of greater China.

Dynastic opposition to the Ch'ing, claiming in part to represent the Ming tradition, continued for a number of decades. One consequence of confrontation with this opposition was the launching of probably the largest war fleet in Chinese history, under Chinese command like the fleets of the Yüan and the Ming, which took Taiwan in 1683. Several hundred thousand refugees had fled to the island since the Manchu invasion and had organized a state on the Chinese pattern. Since total evacuation did not seem practicable, and since it was feared that the island could become a base for foreigners, especially the Dutch and the Spaniards, as it had some decades before, Admiral Shih Lang (1621–96) recommended that it should be incorporated into the empire. After some initial demurring on the part of Manchu dignitaries, this was carried out in 1684.

The suppression of the Mongols, who were another threat to the Manchu, was a protracted struggle. Even before their invasion of China the Manchu had managed to subdue sections of the East Mongols (1634–35). The measures they took to stabilize the situation on the periphery of the empire were the same that the Ming had used against themselves. They allocated specific geographic areas to the separate tribes, confirmed the succession of their princes, bestowed titles and honours on them, permitted a specific volume of trade at fixed market places, compelled the tribes to send tribute regularly and supervised their assemblies. In short, they tried to control their potential enemies by keeping them apart. However, it was not a system that could be applied with any great success to more remote tribes. This became apparent at the very latest when the Dsungars, a branch of the West Mongols (Oirat), who had close secular and spiritual ties with the Lamaist hierarchy in Tibet, overran the Moslem population of the oases of East Turkestan (1678–79) and so formed an agglomerated force which advanced against the East Mongols in 1686 and thus came

160

dangerously close to Peking. The Dsungars' eastward drive was halted in 1696 at the battle of Urga on the Kerulen River. Outer Mongolia and the oasis of Hami were added to the empire, but the situation farther west continued to be threatening, especially when the Dsungars invaded Tibet (1717–18). In consequence, and with the support of the Tibetan nobility, the Ch'ing intervened in Tibet for the first time in 1720. The Manchu protectorate in Tibet was not established, however, until the danger of the Dsungars gaining control of the country revived in 1751. The remnants of the Dsungars were finally wiped out in a last campaign in 1756–57. With that the whole of East Turkestan, the Tarim basin and the region of seven river valleys between the Ili and the Karatal, and as far as the farther shore of Lake Balkhash, fell to the empire. Governors took up residence in Ili and Urumchi to administer the 'New Frontier March' (Hsin-chiang: Sinkiang). The central Asian territories for which the Ch'ing had had to fight for so long, remained their first priority even after they had suffered several setbacks on the coast in the nineteenth century. When Li Hung-chang (1823–1901) wanted to build a fleet to oppose Japan's growing influence in Korea in 1875, he had to give way to Tso Tsung-t'ang (1812–85), who maintained that the defence of the distant north-west frontier near Ili and keeping the Russians at bay were more important.

The Ch'ing empire in the second half of the eighteenth century seemed strategically well-knit and secure. The dynastic opposition had been eliminated, the homelands of the hostile border races were under control, the source of religious fanaticism (Tibet) had been stopped up. Every potentate outside the empire seemed to recognize the dynasty. The realm was encircled by a ring of tributaries: some no more than minor tribes, others relatively large states like Korea. In principle China regarded them all as equals, but there were differences in essential details, for instance in the frequency with which their delegations were received, which was identical with the frequency of opportunities to trade: the Koreans were permitted, or compelled, to come once a year, the Gurkhas of Nepal every five years, the Burmese every ten years. A total of 216 delegations visited Peking between 1662 and 1762, while between 1762 and 1860 there were 254. The Ch'ing were of course forced to recognize that external trade could not be restricted to exchanges with the emissaries bringing tribute, first and foremost because the trading interests of the Chinese themselves could not be channelled through the tribute system. In order to avoid the anomalies of the Ming period, the Ch'ing legalized private

161

foreign trade. They did so without either encouraging it or re-examining the efficacy of the tribute system. Certain commercial houses were appointed official brokers (*kung-hang*: Cohong), and became responsible for the observance of the regulations. Until well into the nineteenth century the system of trade concessions remained as an instrument for obtaining specific political or strategic ends and for ensuring the internal and external stability of the state. The treaties the Ch'ing concluded with the Russians, at Nerchinsk (1689) and Kiatka (1727), illustrate this, with the Ch'ing granting trading concessions in return for the Russian undertaking to respect the territorial integrity of China. At that date the regions to the north and east of Amur and Ussuri were recognized by Russia as belonging to the Manchu empire. In the Sino-Manchurian view the agreement was fully consistent with the tribute system. The Russian trade missions were received in Peking like the delegations of tributary states, their wares were checked and they were sent on their way again. The Russians executed the obligatory kotow before the emperor, but when Chinese emissaries went to Russia (1731–32) they prostrated themselves in the same way before the tzar. This was recognized to be a necessary concession, in order to prevent the Russians from giving any support to the Dsungars. In other words, the Chinese could on occasion bring themselves to be pragmatic in their relations with the rest of the world, as the Sung emperors had already shown. In general, however, the assumption that the position occupied in the world by the Son of Heaven was unique and by definition superior to all others, had found its institutional expression in the tribute system. If China was strong the system was its own justification; if China was weak the outside world was prepared to go along with the system, as long as the trade opportunities bound up with it were attractive. Both sets of circumstances could exist simultaneously on different fronts. But the tribute system was not only a manifestation of the Son of Heaven's pre-eminence in the world, it was also an instrument of legitimization within his own realm. As long as his claim never to have consorted with an equal, that is, with someone who had not kotowed to him, was valid, he could uphold his claim to supreme and sole authority in China too. The tribute system was an outcome and a confirmation of China's special form of absolute monarchy.

The Europeans who appeared at the gates of China in ever-increasing number in the eighteenth century also had to comply with the system. That was all right so long as they were content to take part in the limited, controlled trade and the unlimited illegal trade that was available, under the conditions imposed by China. One of the conditions was that the foreign country must either comport itself as a tributary state, like Portugal, Holland and Russia, or do all its trading through the Cohong, the organization of merchants authorized to engage in foreign trade, like Spain, France, Sweden, Denmark and the English East India Company. Attempts by England to loosen the grip of the Chinese state monopoly failed, not least because ambassadors like Macartney (1793) and Amherst (1816), who came to Peking as the official representatives of their king, refused to prostrate themselves before the emperor in the customary fashion. There was no official interest in foreign trade in China. King George III was informed that the 'Celestial Empire' itself possessed everything in superfluity (1793). Moreover Peking lacked concrete information about any of the European countries: their political system and relationships, their dynamism and recent progress and above all their military power. When the Sino-Manchurian troops were beaten in fighting on the coast by the English, who wanted to force China to import the opium which was vitally important to the economy of British India (1839–40), the court and the civil service were taken completely by surprise by the tactical strength of these 'barbarians'.

This new enemy with his steamships and cannon was stronger than any China had ever had to face before. For the first time the empire had to make concessions at her maritime frontier, which had until then been left in relative peace. The Treaty of Nanking (1842, Supplementary Treaty 1843), the first of the so-called 'Unequal Treaties' (*pu-p'ing-teng t'iao-yüeh*), saw the cession of Hong Kong to England, and enforced the opening of Canton, Amoy, Fuchou, Ningpo and Shanghai as free-trade ports. There was still a compromise in this treaty between the traditional Chinese and the European conceptions of relationships between states. There seemed to be no essential difference between the principle of 'extraterritoriality' and the precedent of the foreign enclaves, with their own administration and laws, that had existed on Chinese soil in the past. The 'most favoured nation' clause, too, which was included in very nearly every bilateral or multilateral treaty from 1843 onwards, was reconcilable with the traditional concept; for all 'barbarians', as a matter of principle, had the same claim on the emperor's favour. Each treaty that followed, however, increasingly undermined the Chinese position. England and France seized on an incident of no great importance as a pretext for renewed military intervention in China in 1857. The Chinese government was forced once more to sign a treaty, the terms of which had been dictated to them. In this, the Treaty of Tientsin (1858), they agreed, among other things, too the accreditation of foreign ambassadors to the capital. Since this practice was totally contrary to the traditional Chinese theory of government and was without precedent in the whole of Chinese history, Chinese officials delayed the exchange of the ratification documents. In order, therefore, to give weight to their position, the English and the French attacked China once more, and their troops entered Peking. Only then was the court prepared to allow the representatives of foreign sovereign states to take up residence in the capital. It was then, if not before, that China's concept began to waver of her own standing *vis-à-vis* the outside world. This extension of European international law to China has been called, somewhat euphemistically, 'China's entry into the family of nations' (C.Y.Hsü); but for China, at that stage, it meant nothing more and nothing less than a gradual relinquishing of her sovereignty. The Chinese hardly understood the European law of nations, and they were not strong enough to hold their own in the system. It was some years before China exercised her right to send ambassadors to the western capitals; not until 1877 was a permanent mission set up in London. Distrust, psychological inhibitions and fear of being discredited in their own country meant that it was only with a heavy heart that Chinese officials went abroad.

So far as the court was concerned, the concessions were simply attempts to keep power in its own hands, in the hope of triumphing finally over the aggressive 'barbarians' in spite of everything. The regions to the east and north of Amur and Ussuri had to be ceded to Russia, in connection with the Treaties of Tientsin and Peking (1860), a limit was imposed on the level of coastal import tariffs, and more ports had to be opened to the foreigners, and there were more blows to come. Russia invaded the Ili region in 1870, and the most important of the tributary states fell one by one to foreign overlords: the Liu-ch'iu islands to Japan (1880), Annam to France (1885), Burma to England (1886) and Korea to Japan (1895). The Korean triumph of Japan, the 'pigmy land' (*wo-kuo*) that owed so much to China, was a particularly bitter blow to the Chinese sense of civilized order. In 1898 the Ch'ing had to 'lease' a whole string of coastal areas at one go to the foreign powers, who also took the precaution of reserving large parts of the empire for themselves as 'spheres of influence'. It is beyond dispute that at the turn of the century China was a semi-colony of the imperial powers, which now included Japan. When a small body of rebels (the Boxers) began to concentrate their actions increasingly against the foreign residents in the late 1890s, some circles at the court saw it as the last chance of salvaging the desperate situation. They supported the rebels and persuaded them to besiege the legation quarter in Peking. An expeditionary force sent by the imperial powers quickly put an end to this uncoordinated, ineffectual rising (1900). The international Boxer Protocol (1901) humiliated China further and laid heavier burdens on her. Besides other conditions, the government had to undertake to pay an indemnity of 450 million silver dollars, spread over a period of forty years. It was ruin for the Ch'ing dynasty, both financially and morally, in the eyes of their Chinese associates.

The collapse of traditional China was initiated from outside, but the apparently possible means of recovery from political collapse were also foreign in inspiration. Those who criticized this development and those who were responsible for the situation failed to realize fully that China was betrayed not merely by military and political weakness but by being in the throes of an all-round social, economic, intellectual and ideological crisis. The early suggestions for modernization put forward by traditionalists were eclectic, uncoordinated and dilettante. Men like Li Hung-chang and Chang Chih-tung (1837–1909) not only believed that a few technical innovations and some modern weaponry would enable China to repay the imperialist powers in their own coin. They also maintained that such means might also overcome the internal political crisis and thus simultaneously maintain the traditional order, which of course included the privileged position of the educated administrative class. The preservation of the essential Chinese identity was from the start central to the debate about 'self-strengthening' (*tzu-ch'iang*), as the first attempts at modernization were called. Chang Chih-tung coined the expression 'Chinese culture as the basis, western teaching for [practical] use' (*Chung-hsüeh wei t'i, Hsi-hsüeh wei yung*). That these cautious modernizers were overruled by more conservative forces, simply illustrates the hopeless stagnation of the situation in which Chinese society now found itself. In a narrower sense the Self-Strengthening policy, which dominated discussion from the early 1860s to the mid-1870s, applied only to military recovery. But it also indirectly encouraged development of individual industries like mining and shipbuilding and the installation, on a modest scale, of modern means of communication. A small number of schools began to teach western languages and natural sciences. Also connected with the Self-Strengthening movement, though at an even further remove, was a not insignificant institutional change. From 1861 foreign affairs were handled by an Office for General Administration of Matters concerning the Various Countries (*tsung-li ko-kuo shih-wu ya-men*, usually referred to as the *Tsungli Yamen* by commentators). It was not a Foreign Office in the western sense – it was not until 1901 that an institution of that nature was set up – but it was an important advance on the traditional 'dealing with barbarian affairs' (*ch'ou-pan i-wu*). More successful adaptation was shown in the diplomatic field than in technology or education, at least for as long as Prince Kung (1835–98) had any influence on policy-making in Peking. His conciliatory policies aimed at restoring peace at home, in the traditional conviction that internal stability would bring peace on the frontiers. He persuaded the government to take a new look at the detested treaties, to recognize that they were an instrument for order that could be made binding on the other signatories too and to make the most of them accordingly.

The Self-Strengthening movement was only the first of China's attempts to adapt. After the Sino-Japanese War (1894–95) proved that even militarily the movement was ineffective, a group of young literati concluded that purely formal adaptation to the practices of the industrial nations would not suffice to check their aggression and preserve China's statehood. They were convinced that 'institutional change' (*kai chih*) and 'legal reform' (*pien fa*) were absolutely essential. The group, which was led by K'ang Yu-wei (1858–1927), Liang Ch'i-ch'ao (1873–1929) and T'an Ssu-t'ung (1865–98), succeeded temporarily in gaining political influence through the young Emperor Te-tsung (1871–1908; known as the Kuang-hsü Emperor) and drew up a programme for reform. In complete conformity with the Confucian tradition, they justified their innovations by references to the literary canon and the official histories, attempting to show that these sanctioned some of the institutions and traditions of the West. However, they at once ran into the opposition of orthodox thought in the lettered classes and the conservative circles at court. Both these parties had good reason to fear for their privileges, in face of the proposed administrative, military and above all fiscal reforms. After 103 days, on 21 September 1898, the 'Old Buddha', Te-tsung's aunt, the Empress Dowager Tzu-hsi (1835–1908), seized control of the government with the aid of the conservatives. Te-tsung was placed in custody, and the reformers had to flee or, like T'an Ssu-t'ung, pay with their lives.

166

The third important initiative to reform and modernize the Chinese state is closely linked with the name of Sun Yat-sen (1866–1925). Sun had founded the 'Society for the Restoration of China' (*Hsing-Chunghui*) in about 1892 and made particular efforts to raise support among Chinese residents abroad. Like earlier reformers he had at first hoped to reach his goals through the dynasty, not in opposition to it. However he soon realized that that was to wish the impossible. He also abandoned at an early stage his plan for turning China into a constitutional monarchy. His movement was to sound the knell, not only for the Manchu dynasty, but for the monarchic system in China altogether. In this connection, it is probably not a random coincidence that Sun Yat-sen, of all the reformers brought up in traditional China, was the one with the greatest experience of the outside world and the most foreign contacts.

Her confrontation with the industrial nations of the world was China's second head-on collision with a fundamentally different civilization. The first, the Mongol conquest, brought her into contact with an expansive nomadic culture. In the nineteenth century the sedentary Chinese society, with its agrarian economy and bureaucratic institutions, came face to face with an expansive industrial culture. To the present day, China is striving to recover from the sense of dislocation arising out of that encounter and, within the continuing confrontation between developed and underdeveloped states, to survive as state and as nation.

Select Bibliography

Select Bibliography

BIBLIOGRAPHIES

Cordier, H. *Bibliotheca Sinica, Dictionnaire bibliographique des ouvrages relatifs à l'empire Chinois*, 5 vols. Paris 1904–8, suppl. Paris 1922–24.

Herman, T. *The Geography of China, A Selected and Annotated Bibliography*. New York 1967.

Hucker, C. O. *China, A Critical Bibliography*. Tucson, Ariz. 1962.

Lust, J., and Eichhorn, W. *Index Sinicus, A Catalogue of Articles Relating to China in Periodicals and Other Collective Publications 1920–1955*. Cambridge 1964.

Schackor, P. E. *Bibliografia Kitaja*. Moscow 1960.

Yüan, T. L. *China in Western Literature, A Continuation of Cordier's Bibliotheca Sinica*. New Haven 1958.

Journal of Asian Studies (previously *Far Eastern Quarterly*), ed. The Association for Asian Studies, Ann Arbor, Mich. (annual bibliography of works relating to China in European languages).

Revue bibliographique de Sinologie, ed. Ecole Pratique des Hautes Etudes, VIe Section, Paris (annual bibliography of works relating to China mainly in Asian languages).

GENERAL WORKS

Eberhard, W. *A History of China*. Berkeley/Los Angeles 1969 (3rd edn, 1st edn, Bern 1948).

Eichhorn, W. *Kulturgeschichte Chinas, Eine Einführung*. Stuttgart 1964.

Elvin, M., *The Pattern of the Chinese Past*, London, 1973.

Fairbank, J. K., Reischauer, E. O., Craig, A. M. *East Asia, The Modern Transformation*. Boston 1965.

Franke, H., and Trauzettel, R. *Das chinesische Kaiserreich*. Frankfurt 1968.

Franke, O. *Geschichte des chinesischen Reiches, Eine Darstellung seiner Entstehung, seines Wesens und seiner Entwicklung bis zur neuesten Zeit*, 5 vols. Berlin 1930–52.

Goodrich, L. C. *A Short History of the Chinese People*. New York 1963 (reprint 3rd edn, 1st edn 1943).

Levenson, J. R., and Schurmann, F. R. *China, An Interpretative History*. Berkeley/Los Angeles 1969.

Needham, J. *Science and Civilization in China*. Cambridge 1961–.

Reischauer, E. O., and Fairbank, J. K. *East Asia, The Great Tradition*. Boston 1958, London 1961.

Tung, C. M. *An Outline History of China*. Peking 1959 (2nd edn).

HISTORIOGRAPHY

China's History Through European Eyes

Dawson, R. *The Chinese Chameleon, An Analysis of European Conceptions of Chinese Civilization*. London 1967.

Franke, O. 'Wie und zu welchem Zweck studiert man chinesische Geschichte' in *Der Orient in deutscher Forschung*. Leipzig 1944, 105–16.

Grimm, T. 'Unsere Erfassung des ostasiatischen Geschichtsprozesses', in *Saeculum*, 14 (1963), 47–52.

Lach, D. F. *Asia in the Making of Europe*. Chicago 1965.

Mason, M. G. *Western Concepts of China and the Chinese, 1840–76*. New York 1939.

Reichwein, A. *China and Europe, Intellectual and Artistic Contacts in the Eighteenth Century*. London/New York 1925.

Historiography and the Chinese Historical Consciousness

Beasley, W. G., and Pulleyblank, E. G. (eds.) *Historians of China and Japan*. London 1965 (1st edn 1961).

Feuerwerker, A. (ed.) *History in Communist China*. Cambridge, Mass. 1968.

Franke, O. 'Der Sinn der chinesischen Geschichtsschreibung' in *Sinologische Arbeiten*, 3 (1945), 96–113.

Gardener, C. S. *Chinese Traditional Historiography*. Cambridge, Mass. 1961 (1st edn 1938).

Grimm, T. 'Idee und Wirklichkeit in der chinesischen Geschichte' in *Saeculum*, 10 (1959), 186–95.

Haenisch, E. 'Das Ethos der chinesischen Geschichtsschreibung' in *Saeculum*, 1 (1950), 11–123.

Harrison, J. P. *The Communists and Chinese Peasant Rebellions, A Study in the Rewriting of History*. New York 1969.

Koh, B. 'Zur Werttheorie in der chinesischen Historiographie aufgrund des Shih-t'ung des Liu Chih-chi (661–721)' in *Oriens Extremus*, 4 (1957), 5–21, 128–81.

Schwartz, B. 'A Marxist Controversy in China' in *Far Eastern Quarterly*, 13 (1954), 143–53.

Sung, S. 'The Study of History in Communist China' in *Chinese Culture*, 10 (1969), 15–51.

Teng, S. Y. 'Chinese Historiography in the Last Fifty Years' in *Far Eastern Quarterly*, 8 (1949), 131–56.

The Periodization of Chinese History

Cameron, M. E. 'The Periodization of Chinese History' in *Pacific Historical Review* 15 (1946), 171–77.

Meskill, J. *The Pattern of Chinese History, Cycles, Development or Stagnation*. Boston 1965.

Yang, L. S. 'Toward a Study of Dynastic Configurations in Chinese History' in *idem, Studies in Chinese Institutional History*. Cambridge, Mass. (1961), 1–16.

GEOGRAPHY

Physical Character of the Historical Region

Cressey, G. B. *Land of the 500 Million.* New York 1955.

Herrmann, A. *An Historical Atlas of China.* New edn, Chicago 1966 (1st edn *Historical and Commercial Atlas of China.* Cambridge, Mass. 1935).

Pauels, H. *China, Informationen zur politischen Bildung 96, 99.* Bonn 1961, 1962.

Sellmann, R. R. *An Outline Atlas of Eastern History.* London 1954.

Historical Expansion of the Chinese Empire

Bielenstein, H. 'The Chinese Colonisation of Fukien Until the End of the T'ang' in *Studia Serica B. Karlgren dedicata,* Copenhagen 1959, 98–122.

Bishop, C. W. 'The Geographical Factor in the Development of Chinese Civilization', in *The Geographical Review,* 12 (1922), 19–41.

—— 'The Rise of Civilization in China with Reference to its Geographical Aspects' in *The Geographical Review,* 22 (1932), 617–31.

Boodberg, P. A. 'Two Notes on the History of the Chinese Frontier' in *Harvard Journal of Asian Studies,* 3/4 (1936), 283–307.

Buchanan, K. *The Transformation of the Chinese Earth, Aspects of the Evaluation of the Chinese Earth from the Earliest Times to Mao Tse-tung.* New York 1970.

Chatley, H. 'The Yellow River as a Factor in the Development of China' in *The Asiatic Review,* Jan. 1939, 1–8.

Chi, C. T. *Key Economic Areas in Chinese History, As Revealed in the Development of Public Works for Water-Control,* New York 1963 (1st edn London 1936).

Eberhard, W. *Kultur und Siedlung der Randvölker Chinas.* Leiden 1942.

Lattimore, O. *Inner Asian Frontiers of China.* Boston 1962.

—— *Studies in Frontier History, Collected Papers 1929–1958.* London 1962.

Roxby, P. M. 'The Expansion of China' in *Scottish Geographical Magazine,* 46 (1960), 65–80.

Watson, B. *The Frontier of China, A Historical Guide.* New York 1966.

Wiens, H. *China's March Towards the Tropics.* Hamden 1954.

Wiethoff, B. *Chinas dritte Grenze, Der traditionelle chinesische Staat und der küstennahe Seeraum.* Wiesbaden 1969.

DEMOGRAPHY

Archaeological Finds and Ancient Traditions

Chang, K. C. *The Archeology of China.* New Haven 1968 (1st edn 1963).

Cheng, T. K. *Archaeology in China.* Cambridge 1959–.

Creel, H. G. *A Survey of the Formative Period of Chinese Civilization.* Chicago 1964 (1st edn London 1936).

Eberhard, W. *Lokalkulturen im alten China,* 2 vols. Leiden/Peking 1942.

173

Haloun, G. 'Beiträge zur Siedlungsgeschichte chinesischer Clans' in *Asia Major Hirth Anniversary Volume* (1923), 165–81.

Karlgren, B. 'Legends and Cults in Ancient China' in *Bulletin of the Museum of Far Eastern Antiquities*, 18 (1946), 199–366.

Maspero, H. *La Chine antique*. Paris 1955 (1st edn 1927).

Watson, W. *China Before the Han Dynasty*. New York 1961.

—— *Early Civilization in China*. London 1966.

Population and Society

Bielenstein, H. 'The Census of China During the Period 2–742 A.D.' in *Bulletin of the Museum of Far Eastern Antiquities*, 19 (1947), 125–63.

Chang, C. L. *The Chinese Gentry, Studies on Their Role in Nineteenth Century Chinese Society*. Seattle 1955.

—— *The Income of the Chinese Gentry*. Seattle 1962.

Eberhard, W. *Social Mobility in Traditional China*. Leiden 1961.

Eichhorn, W. 'Gesamtbevölkerungsziffern des Sung-Reiches' in *Oriens Extremus*, 4 (1957), 52–69.

Friese, H. 'Zum Aufstieg von Handwerkern ins Beamtentum während der Ming-Zeit' in *Oriens Extremus*, 6 (1959), 160–76.

Giles, L. 'A Census of Tun-huang' in *T'oung Pao*, 16 (1915), 468–88.

Ho, P. T. 'The Salt Merchants of Yang chou, A Study of Commercial Capitalism in 18th Century China' in *Harvard Journal of Asian Studies*, 17 (1954), 130–68.

—— *Studies on the Population of China, 1368–1953*. Cambridge, Mass. 1959.

—— *The Ladder of Success in Imperial China, Aspects of Social Mobility, 1368–1911*. London 1962.

Hsu, C. Y. *Ancient China in Transition, An Analysis of Social Mobility, 722–222*. Stanford, Ca. 1965.

Kato, S. 'On the Hang or the Association of Merchants in China' in *Memoirs of the Research Department of the Toyo Bunko*, 8 (1936), 45–83.

Lang, O. *Chinese Family and Society*. New York 1968 (1st edn New Haven 1948).

Pulleyblank, E. G. 'Registration of Population in China in the Sui and T'ang Periods' in *Journal of the Economic and Social History of the Orient*, 4, 3 (1961), 289–301.

—— 'The Origins and Nature of Chattel Slavery in China' in *Journal of the Economic and Social History of the Orient*, 1, 2 (1958), 185–220.

Wittfogel, K. A. *Wirtschaft und Gesellschaft, Versuch der wissenschaftlichen Analyse einer großen asiatischen Agrargesellschaft*. Leipzig 1931.

POLARITIES AND TENSIONS

Centre and Periphery

Balazs, E. 'Beiträge zur Wirtschaftsgeschichte der T'ang-Zeit' in *Mittellungen des Seminars für orientalische Sprachen*, 34 (1931), 1–92; 35 (1932), 1–73; 36 (1933), 1–62.

Balazs, E. *Chinese Civilization and Bureaucracy, Variations on a Theme.* New Haven/London 1964.

—— *Political Theory and Administrative Reality.* London 1965.

Bishop, J. L. (ed.) *Studies of Governmental Institutions in Chinese History.* Cambridge, Mass. 1968.

Bodde, D. *China's First Unifier.* Hong Kong 1967 (1st edn Leiden 1938).

Ch'en, K. S. *Buddhism in China, A Historical Survey.* Princeton 1964

Ch'u, T. T. *Law and Society in Traditional China.* Paris/Leiden 1961.

Crawford, R. B. 'Eunuch Power in the Ming Dynasty' in *T'oung Pao*, 49 (1961), 115–48.

Escarra, J. *Le droit chinois.* Paris 1936.

Fairbank, J. K. (ed.) *Chinese Thought and Institutions.* Chicago 1957.

Franke, H. *Geld und Wirtschaft unter der Mongolenherrschaft.* Leipzig 1949.

Gernet, J. *Les aspects économiques du bouddhisme dans la société chinoise du Ve au Xe siècle.* Saigon 1956.

Huston, H. C. *The Grain Tribute System of China.* Cambridge, Mass. 1956.

Kaltenmark, M. *Lao Tzu and Taoism.* Stanford, Ca. 1969 (1st edn Paris 1956).

Parsons, J. B. *A Preliminary Analysis of the Ming Dynasty Bureaucracy.* Kyoto 1959.

Schurmann, F. R. *Economic Structure of the Yüan Dynasty.* Cambridge, Mass. 1956.

Shryock, J. K. *The Origin and Development of the State Cult of Confucius.* New York 1922.

Swann, N. L. *Food and Money in Ancient China, The Earliest Economic History of China, to A.D 25.* Princeton 1950.

Twitchett, D. C. *Financial Administration under the T'ang Dynasty.* Cambridge 1963.

Weber-Schäfer, P. *Oikumene und Imperium, Studien zur Ziviltheologie des chinesischen Kaiserreiches.* München 1968.

Wright, A. F. *Buddhism in Chinese History.* Stanford, Ca. 1959.

Wright, A. F., and Nivison, D. S. *Confucianism in Action.* Stanford, Ca. 1959.

Wright, A. F. (ed.) *The Confucian Persuasion.* Stanford, Ca. 1960.

Yang, L. S. *Money and Credit in China, A Short History.* Cambridge, Mass. 1952.

The Rulers and the Ruled

Ch'ü, T. T. *Local Government in China under the Ch'ing.* Cambridge, Mass. 1962.

Eberhard, W. *Conquerors and Rulers, Social Forces in Medieval China.* Leiden 1965 (1st edn 1952).

Eichhorn, W. 'Zur Vorgeschichte des Aufstandes von Wang Hsiao-po und Li Shun in Szuch'uan (993–995)' in *Zeitschrift der Deutschen Morgenländischen Gesellschaft*, 105 (1955), 192–209.

Haenisch, E. 'Der Aufstand des Ch'en She im Jahre 209 v. Chr.' in *Asia Major*, 2 NS (1951), 71–84.

Hsiao, K. C. *Rural China, Imperial Control in the Nineteenth Century.* Seattle/London 1967 (1st edn Seattle 1960).

Kao, Y. K. 'A Study of the Fang La Rebellion' in *Harvard Journal of Asian Studies*, 24 (1962/63), 17–63.

Lee, J. S. 'The Periodic Recurrence of Internecine Wars in China' in *China Journal of Science and Arts*, 14 (1931), 111–14, 159–63.

Levy, H. S. *Biography of Huang Ch'ao*. Berkeley 1955.

—— 'Yellow Turban Religion and Rebellion at the End of Han' in *Journal of the American Oriental Society*, 76 (1956), 214–27.

Michael, F., and Chang, C. L. *The Taiping Rebellion, History and Documents*. Seattle/London 1966.

Parsons, J. B. *The Peasant Rebellions of the Late Ming Dynasty*. Tucson, Ariz. 1970.

Purcell, V. *The Boxer Uprising, A Background Study*. Cambridge 1963.

Rawlinson, R. 'A Study of the Rebellions of China' in *Chinese Recorder*, 36 (1905), 107–17.

Shih, Y. C. 'Some Chinese Rebel Ideologies' in *T'oung Pao*, 44 (1956), 150–226.

Taylor, G. E. 'The Taiping Rebellion – Its Economic Background and Social Theory' in *Chinese Social and Political Review*, 16 (1953), 545–614.

Teng, S. Y. 'A Political Interpretation of Chinese Rebellions and Revolutions' in *Tsing Hwa Journal of Chinese Studies*, NS 1 (1958), 91–119.

—— *The Nien Army and Their Guerilla Warfare. 1851–1868*. Paris/Leiden 1961.

China and the Outside World

Cordier, H. *Histoire des relations de la Chine avec les puissances occidentales 1860–1902*. 3 vols., Paris 1901–2.

Fairbank, J. K. *Trade and Diplomacy on the China Coast, The Opening of the Treaty Ports 1842 to 1854*. 2 vols., Cambridge, Mass. 1953.

—— (ed.) *The Chinese World Order, Traditional China's Foreign Relations*. Cambridge, Mass. 1968.

Fitzgerald, C. P. *The Chinese View of Their Place in the World*. New York/London/Toronto 1964.

Franke, W. *China und das Abendland*. Göttingen 1962.

Hsü, J. C. Y. *China's Entrance into the Family of Nations, The Diplomatic Phase 1858–1880*. Cambridge, Mass. 1960.

Morse, H. B. *International Relations of the Chinese Empire*. 3 vols, London 1910–18.

Pelliot, P. 'Les grands voyages maritimes chinois au début du XVe siècle' in *T'oung Pao*, 30 (1933), 237–452; 31 (1935), 274–314; 32 (1936), 210–22.

Petech, L. *China and Tibet in the Early 18th Century*. Leiden 1950.

Purcell, V. *The Chinese in South-East Asia*. London 1965 (1st edn 1951).

Rockhill, W. W. *China's Intercourse with Korea from the 15th Century to 1895*. London 1905.

Schafer, E. H. *The Golden Peaches of Samarkand, A Study of T'ang Exotics*. Berkeley/Los Angeles 1963.

—— *The Vermillion Bird, T'ang Images of the South*. Berkeley/Los Angeles 1967.

Teng, S. Y. and Fairbank, J. K. *China's Response to the West, A*

Documentary Survey 1839–1923. Cambridge, Mass. 1954.

Wang, I. T. *Official Relations between China and Japan 1368–1549.* Cambridge, Mass. 1953.

Wiethoff, B. *Die chinesische Seeverbotspolitik und der private*

Überseehandel von 1368 bis 1567. Hamburg 1963.

Yü, Y. S. *Trade and Expansion in Han China, A Study in the Structure of Sino-Barbarian Relations.* Berkeley/Los Angeles 1967.

Chronological Table

			(*Capital city: modern name*)
c. 2000–1500 BC	Hsia dynasty (legendary?)		
c. 1500–1000 BC	Shang dynasty		Anyang
c. 1000–249 BC	Chou dynasty		
c. 1000–771 BC	Former (Western) Chou		Sian
771–249 BC	Later (Eastern) Chou		Loyang
771–481 BC	Spring and Autumn period		
480–221 BC	Time of the Warring States		
221–207 BC	Ch'in dynasty	First unification of the empire	Sian
206 BC–AD 220	Han dynasty		
206 BC–AD 8	Former Han		Sian
9–AD 23	Wang Mang interregnum		
25–AD 220	Later Han		Loyang
220–80	Three Kingdoms	First division of the empire	
220–65	Wei		Loyang
221–65	Shu Han		Chengtu
222–80	Wu		Nanking
265–419	Chin dynasty	Second unification of the empire	
265–317	Western Chin		Loyang
317–420	Eastern Chin		Nanking
420–81	Southern and Northern dynasties	Second division of the empire	
386–543	Wei dynasty		Alien dynasty: Toba
581–618	Sui dynasty	Third unification of the empire	Sian
618–906	T'ang dynasty		Sian/Loyang
907–60	Five dynasties	Third division of the empire	
937–1125	Liao dynasty		Alien dynasty: Kitan
960–1279	Sung dynasty	Fourth unification of the empire	
960–1126	Northern Sung		Kaifeng
1127–1279	Southern Sung		Hangchou
990–1227	Hsi-Hsia		Alien dynasty: Tangut-Tibetans
1115–1234	Chin dynasty		Alien dynasty: Jurchen
1260–1367	Yüan dynasty		Peking Alien dynasty: Mongols
1368–1644	Ming dynasty		Nanking/Peking
1644–1912	Ch'ing dynasty		Peking Alien dynasty: Manchu
1912, 12 Feb.	Imperial government resigns		

Index

Index

Polo, Marco 9, 10, 48, 100, 149
population 58–69, 110; control 61–2
porcelain: state manufacture 69
Port Arthur 47
Portuguese 163; in Macao 144, 156
Poyanghu, Lake 38
Privy State Council 94, 99

RECORDS OF CURRENT GOVERNMENT (*shih-cheng chi*) 21
Records of the Historian (*Shih-chi*) 19–20, 56
Red Eyebrows (*Ch'ih-mei*) 83, 117
religion 11, 65
Ricci, Matteo 11, 156
rice 33, 34, 35–7, 60, 61, 95
Romance of the Three Kingdoms (*San-kuo yen-i*) 102
Russia 61, 163; publications on China 12; territories ceded to 47, 164; treaties 162, 164; 1870 invasion 164; *and see* Soviet Union

SALT trade 119, 120; *and see* state monopolies
Saracens 100
Sayan mts 34
scripts 18, 53, 76, 138; inscriptions 18–19, 24, 53, 54; Sanskrit 143
Second World War 17, 18, 48
Secret societies 116–26, 129, 158
Shang dynasty 30, 139; historiography 20, 24, 27; fall 28; domains 38; genealogy 53; culture and society 53–5, 63, 65; origins 57
Shanghai 126, 163
Shang Yang 75, 76, 112

Shansi 33, 38, 52, 73, 85, 128; crops 37; weather 37
Shantung 34, 37, 38, 47, 61, 72, 83, 117, 121, 124, 129, 131; crops 35, 36; weather 35, 36
Shan-yüan, treaty of 146
Shensi 33, 44, 52, 54, 71, 74, 85, 87, 106, 124–5, 129; crops 36; population 58–9; River 36, 38, 39; weather 36
Shen-tsung 95
Shih Lang 160
Shih-tsung (Yung-chen Emperor) 108–9
Shipping Authorities 148, 154
Shu dynasty 84; state 39, 49, 74
Shun dynasty 124
Siberia 33
Sichota-Alin mts 34
Sikiang River 37
silk 154; state manufacture 69
Silk Road 143
Silla (Korea) 42, 144
Sinkiang (Hsin-chiang) 46, 47, 161; drops 36–7; weather 36–7
Sino-Japanese War 111, 166
slavery/slaves 30, 56, 58, 83, 116
Society for the Restoration of China 167
Society of Jesus *see* Jesuits
Society of the Worshippers of God 127
'son of heaven' 72, 142, 146, 148, 153, 162
Soviet Union: confrontation with China 17; study of China 18, 30
soya beans 35–6
Spain 160, 163
Spencer: *Study of Sociology* 24

Spring and Autumn (*Ch'un-ch'iu*) 72, 81
Ssechuan 39, 46, 47, 84, 85, 106, 117, 124–5, 152; crops 36; population 58, 59, 60; River 36, 37, 50; weather 36
Ssu-ma Ch'ien 20, 53, 56; *and see Records of the Historian*
Ssu-ma Kuang 49; *Comprehensive Mirror* (*Tzu-chih t'ung-chien*) 19, 21
Ssu-ma T'an 20; *and see Records of the Historian*
state monopolies 76, 134; alcohol 79, 92; minting 79; iron 72, 79; salt 72, 79, 92; tea 92
Suchou 60
Sui dynasty 29, 42, 47–8, 59, 87–90, 119, 142
Sun Ch'üan 84
Sun Yat-sen 111, 114, 132, 167
Sung dynasty 29, 30, 31, 45, 66, 98, 101, 102, 103, 111, 125, 134, 151, 152; historiography 22; empire 43; relations with Kitan 44, 147; capital at Kaifeng 48, 49; urbanization 60; examinations 67; trade 68–9; civil service 68–9; origins 93; administration, centralization 93–8; reforms 95–6, 113; internal stability 145; treaties 146; overcome by Kublai Khan 149
Sung, Northern 45, 96, 97, 121
Sung, Southern 44, 49, 96–7, 99, 121, 147–8, 150, 154